SPAM

2

SCAM

How 2 B e-*SAFE*

RamPad

Published in association with

CreateSpace

100 Enterprise Way
Scotts Valley, CA 95066 USA

www.createspace.com

ISBN   1 440424 61 6
EAN/ISBN-13   9 781440 424618

RamPad, 1961-

SPAM 2 SCAM How 2 B e-SAFE

(https://www.createspace.com/3355182)

Internet, SPAM, e-mail SCAMs, illustrated examples, security basics, choosing a strong password, FAQ and further resources.

Printed in the United States of America by CreateSpace.

DEDICATED TO

All vulnerable *netizens* out there who may benefit from this book to protect their identity from theft, ensure their safety from e-mail SCAMS and safeguard their interests from online frauds.

< 3 >

DISCLAIMER

This book contains some e-mail messages that the Author received in his e-mail inbox and which he cites as examples for what *may* constitute SPAM and/or SCAMs. However, he explicitly states that he does not assert, suggest or insinuate that those names contained in those said copies of e-mails whether that is of any corporations, organisations, government bodies or individuals, are of suspect in any sense or in any manner whatsoever. The Author wishes to emphasise that any names appearing in such SPAM could have been *spoofed*. The Author is only happy to remove any such spoofed name(s) and/or e-mail addresses that appear in those examples with due sympathies. The Author can only request that such incidents be brought to his attention for correction with a copy of a letter to the ISP or authorities as appropriate; however he does not assume any liability for any inconvenience, angst or distress caused to anyone. Once thus notified, the sole responsibility of the Author is to arrange for the removal of any such names or references from the publication of this book promptly and in a timeframe as much as practicable or issue 'errata' in further editions as appropriate. It is in good faith and with good intentions to be of help to readers that he presents them in this book as is and as they arrived in his mail box albeit with explanatory notes on the patterns identified therein. The exception is that for those e-mail addresses that were listed against the 'To:' and/or 'Cc:' fields. They have been removed when appropriate to protect the privacy of the recipients and some changes were made to highlight the patterns and/or as part of formatting. Further, this book is meant for information only and no guarantees, warrantees or indemnity, whatsoever to be assumed, constructed or expected as a result of any unexpected results arising from following any suggestions described in this book in any sections under any heading. Readers are encouraged to seek professional help and technical consultation on how to incorporate them in their specific situation(s) and/or when in doubt before embarking on any experiments based on the contents of this book. The Author further states that he does not claim, suggest or imply in any way that the resources or references that he lists in this book and in turn their respective owners or agencies represented by them, endorsed the contents of this book or its publication, or are associated with the publication of this book in any way.

< 4 >

ACKNOWLWDGEMENTS

The Author wishes to acknowledge all trade marks, copy rights and other intellectual property or proprietary rights of the owners of the respective products, services and ideas mentioned in this book. I gratefully acknowledge my teachers for shaping my intellect, guiding my learning and above all kindling that inquisitiveness to seek knowledge. I acknowledge the books, articles, journals that I read so far and their respective owners for the information that they provided. I acknowledge every act of love, affection and support that I received from family, friends, relatives and strangers that reinforce my trust in humanity. I acknowledge the challenges that came my way that taught me the value of perseverance. I acknowledge every opportunity that tested my mettle in someway or other that provided me with valuable experience. I acknowledge the SPAM that I received over the years, which form the theme of this book. Finally, I acknowledge the presence of an ineffable divine creativity in everything and everyone around us, which keeps our curiosity ever alive.

< 5 >

Table of Contents

< 7 >

< 8 >

Preface

According to web reports quoting the FBI's Internet Crime Report for 2007, total loss from cases of fraud in the US went from USD 185 million to over USD 239 million between 2005 and 2007. That is over 25% increase ! The Sydney Morning Herald reported [1] that Australians lose about AUD 36 million every year in online frauds alone. A study quoted in the same article estimates that *Nigerian* SCAMs cost British economy around GBP 150 million a year. According to reports attributed to Gartner, losses as a result of *phishing* SCAMs alone could top USD 4 billion mark in 2008 !

Security experts at Microsoft estimated [2] that e-mail and instant messaging SCAMs increased by 10% in 2007 compared to that in 2006 and predicted an even more increase in 2008. To deal with the menace of SPAM, global IT cost rose from USD 20.5 billion in 2003 to USD 198 billion by 2007 [3]. The cost of lost productivity globally is further estimated at USD 50 billion.

The statistics as given above is not to alarm but to awaken us to the enormity of the menace. Scammers lead their target(s) to believe that they have won millions from a non-existent lottery; landed a lucrative overseas job but nothing more than collectors of money for the scammers; or secured a *fake* loan, grant, bursary, scholarship or financial assistance on unbelievably attractive terms despite without any paperwork until then. The victims are generally believed to be naïve, technically illiterate or overly trusting. But this is not true. People from all walks of life fall victims to SCAMs. It is sometimes difficult to convince a potential victim that what he/she was relying on was just a SCAM.

This book is not about how to *fight* SPAM by *targeting* spammers. That is the responsibility of law enforcement agencies. Many countries have embarked on that responsibility admirably well. Yet the *net* is becoming

< 9 >

wider without any signs of relief, and there is no place for complacency. Security is not only about hardware, software and/or some rules. It is also about diligent implementation of a plan and regular assessment of its efficacy. That is only possible through increased awareness of the *modus operandi* of the criminals in advance and taking enough precautions proactively. I trust this book will help readers in that.

You may ask why another book ? Aren't there enough material on the *web* already, warning about all these SCAMs ? Certainly, there are. However, rarely – if ever – people end up reading them *until* it is too late. More over, much of such information available on the web is written by experts. To understand them, one needs a minimum level of *technical* knowledge as well, in addition to a high level of comprehension of the English language. To put them into perspective one may need a bit of experience too.

My education and years of experience in the academia, industry and government exposed me to a variety of ICT environments. As a result, I understand what the experts say about the problems and their solutions reasonably well. This enabled me to understand the issues from a technical as well as *user* perspective. In this book, I attempt to translate that learning in a way that may be useful to an average technically-illiterate *netizen*. What follows is therefore my opinion or view formed from such a broad-based background.

In essence, this book attempts to provide some background information to expose readers to the world out there. Exposure can awaken awareness and help build his/her knowledge base. With awareness comes increased alertness; alertness enhances power of observation; and observation leads to recognition of patterns of interest and improves discernment. After recognising a situation for its potential consequences, one can make an *informed* decision to continue the journey or change course as a correction. In most cases that alone will

< 10 >

save any unnecessary heartache much later that would have ensued, had one continued unknowingly.

When I started writing this book, I had in mind my niece who is in year 11 and net savvy, as the targeted audience. Then I added my sister who is not net savvy but well educated. Slowly, I expanded the demographics of my targeted audience constantly. So, I have consciously tried to construct my paragraphs in such a way that most of them come within a *Flesch-Kincaid* grade of close to 10. Further, I tried to make it *non-technical* and easy to comprehend for any reader.

However, in a book of this kind where use of technology forms the theme, it is next to impossible to fully avoid all technical words or expressions. I have tried to limit the use of such terms and used them only when none other would suffice. There is a glossary at the end to explain such terms that are used in this book as a further help to readers. I trust that I have been successful in catering to all vulnerable *netizens* to some extent.

While I have taken utmost care to check, double-check and crosscheck whatever I have written in this book, I do not claim that everything is perfect and/or accurate beyond reproach. Please feel free to point out if anything is incorrect or has a potential of being misunderstood. I will definitely appreciate that.

As a further note, readers will find a 'space' before the exclamation mark (!) in this book. This is only deliberately placed to prevent it from being mistaken for the letter 'l' by anyone, for example people with impaired vision, particularly the elderly. To give company, I have placed the question mark (?) also likewise throughout this book. For those readers who are not familiar with conventions on 'referencing', the number in square brackets as appearing in this book points to the corresponding number as listed under 'References' on page 127.

< 11 >

Introduction

Sometime back, I received an e-mail from my nephew announcing that he found a new job. He is an information and communications technology (ICT) professional. He had signed up on a job board with his Curriculum Vitae (CV) and an IT firm offered him a job in the US without even an interview. But that was normal in those days of IT boom. He wrote: *"The training is in Paris for 90 days and* [I] *need* [to pay] *fees for processing...."*.

Alarm bells started ringing in my head from the *'fees for processing'* part. Such offers are known as *Advance Fee fraud*. I had read about a story of another *netizen* from India for whom everything went so horribly wrong with a similar job offer over the *net*. The news reported that some firm offered that *victim* a job in the UK based on his details that was posted on an international job site. The conditions were unbelievably generous even for a citizen of the UK, but the victim had never worked overseas to spot the allurement. As advised in the mail, at first he made contacts through e-mails and subsequently seemed to have spoken with the people over telephone. Then demands started coming in for money under various heads endlessly one after another. They were apparently for fees such as to verify his qualification, process his visa, prepare a contract of offer, etc. It was an Advance Fee fraud.

By the time the victim realised that he was taken for a ride, he had already paid up an amount roughly equal to USD 25,000.00 and still without any job offer in writing – other than the e-mail – or visa papers. It was too late. It was not an insignificant amount of money for any average citizen of India. The law enforcement agencies could only find out that the bank accounts to which he remitted money online were all promptly closed after a few days of remittal. The con-artist(s) had cleverly wiped out every trace of their tracks. Out of disappointment, guilt and shame he ended up committing suicide, the report said.

< 12 >

A quick check on the name of the employer in my nephew's e-mail turned out that it was phoney. The street address was that of a legal practice in New York. The job offer *appeared* a SCAM. Fortunately, he did not get further entrapped into that web of deceit, a potential Advance Fee Fraud. My nephew was lucky. But according to media reports [4] a well known poet in Australia was not. So were many others in many countries. There are many vulnerable people out there still. This book is written for them.

After learning about my nephew's experience, I kept an interest on e-mail SCAMs and wanted to warn my friends and relatives with details. When I registered on a job board, I was asked to *validate* my e-mail address as part of their process. *Voila* ! Within a short while, my e-mail inbox got flooded with all sorts of e-SCAMs – at the rate of 30 on some days – which one should be aware of. I can not point my fingers to any particular job site because many people, some pretending to be prospective employers perhaps, may scan such sites. More over someone could obtain e-mail addresses in a variety of other means (see discussion under FAQ 8) too.

You may ask what this fuss is all about. Are we not protected by laws of the land ? Yes, we are; for all academic discussions perhaps. Most often the reality is different. Victims, very rarely if ever, complain. The law enforcement agencies can not do anything when scammers clean every trace of their activities even if someone complained. Then in some countries their political masters intervene. *"I do not know how it is in your country, but here in .... it is the well-resourced that wins litigation always"*, a very senior executive of a non-government organisation (NGO) said to me once in a different context. However, that is true in many countries and in many contexts. Most often victims get short-changed by the *system*.

A deception is a deception, a fraud and a SCAM whether it was committed by a scammer, another netizen or a government agency. It

< 13 >

may or may not diminish a person's worth in financial terms but invariably affect his/her dignity adversely for sure. Legal systems have their own course to run, though. Again in another context, an experienced legal professional remarked to me once, *"What we have is a legal system and not a justice system"*. Getting justice may often be more difficult than winning a real lottery irrespective of the merits of the case.

After all that, it could be emotionally draining for a victim to sit through the legal system, which prosecutes to conclude the matter *completely and finally* even if anyone were to be found *accountable*. How would you feel at the end if the honourable court deemed that the victim did not come to the court with a *clean* hand because you failed to take *reasonable* precautions in the first place ? That will be devastating, right ? In effect, I believe that is what pretty much happened once in a case with which I have direct experience. But that is for another time perhaps in another book as that case was not related to e-mail SCAMs.

Statistics too show a low rate of conviction of SCAM artists if media reports are anything to go by. Some activists complain about a lack of Internet-specific legislation. If passing some legislation alone eliminated unacceptable behaviour, then cases of rapes, domestic violence, discrimination, harassment, victimisation or crimes of many other kinds would have stopped, wouldn't they ? In most countries legislators are significantly influenced by lobby groups. The business lobbies could oppose anything that reduces their profit and instead will argue for self regulation. Self regulation is wonderful and perhaps works in most cases. According to a reference listed at Wikipedia [5] there are some spammer-friendly businesses in some countries. You get the picture.

No, I am not building a conspiracy theory here. Nor am I suggesting that it is *futile* to complain or participate in litigations to apprehend criminals. Let me make it clearer. I strongly believe that it is our civic

< 14 >

duty to cooperate with law enforcement agencies in whatever capacities we can and to prevent similar things happening again to another victim. My point is that all such steps are *in response* to a crime that has already *been* committed. There is an important step that anyone can – and I believe should – take much *before*. That is to *prevent* getting into such SCAMs *as far as possible* and that is the subject matter of this book.

So, to use a cliché, *prevention is better than cure*. To use another cliché perhaps, *at the end of the day* it all reverts back to each netizen. It is *left* to us in all probabilities, within the legal and constitutional framework of the country where we live, to ensure our safety, safeguard our interests and protect our identity from theft.

Those of you who attended a Sunday-school might remember the routine there. The Pastor will say, "*Let us all turn to page 'x' in the Holy book*". Then he will ask you whether you are there at page 'x'. After a while waiting for you to turn to that page, he will announce, "… *today we will read on page 'x' about* …….." The first announcement of the page number is to wake you up. You may have been compensating for the lost sleep from the previous night. The second announcement of the page is to let you know the page number that he was going to read out. And the third and last repetition of the page number is before he actually starts reading the text.

You will notice that I have followed more or less a similar approach in this book. If you find that I repeat things, it is only with the same intent i.e., to *wake you up* first to the world out there; then to take you to the *same* page as others; and finally to read out the principles that the text could *help* you with. Those of you, who are already woken up by SPAM or similar experiences from this world of the Internet, please bear with me. This book is for the sake of others who may still be asleep albeit at varying degrees.

< 15 >

This book starts with some basic topics that will give readers a brief description of the background and framework of e-mail services. Then it presents an overview of SPAM in general. The next ten sections deal specifically with SCAMs, describing those variants mostly in circulation. These sections help readers familiarise with some *commonly found patterns* in such e-mails and identify them for what they are; SCAMs. For additional samples of similar e-mails, readers are encouraged to visit some of the resources listed at the end of this book. They should help you practise spotting those identifiable patterns further.

Then the book explores some basic ideas to secure your information environment. It presents a framework and some suggestions to choose passwords. To answer some of the questions that might arise while reading this book, I have also provided some discussion at the end under 'Frequently Asked questions' (FAQ). Finally I have incorporated a quiz under 'Check your VQ' mainly for fun but could be educative too.

Why so many illustrated examples, you may ask. Many times, I have heard people commenting: *"You are right. All the online lotteries that you mentioned may be SCAMs. But see, this is an online promotion. You don't have to sign up here. It is written right here"*. Then there are allurements of various kinds in SCAM-mails; professedly to share what is *claimed* as someone else's will, unlawfully obtained wealth or unknown accounts; all under a series of false pretexts but very convincing to many !

Detective Superintendent Brian Hay, from Queensland Police fraud squad in Australia was reported [1] to have observed that he got phone calls regularly seeking his help from concerned people, who suspected that their mother or father could be a victim of a scam but were unable to convince them. Isn't it an irony of sorts that we are so naïve to the extent of trusting a stranger far away; but at the same time overly suspicious of relatives, friends or someone nearby ! No wonder why human beings are considered as walking contradictions ! From those

< 16 >

examples of many variants of the same type of e-mails here in this book, I trust that people will be able to see the game *clearly* for what it is. This book is intended to help them shed any such illusion that just because a fraudster says that their victim(s) did not have to sign up or buy any tickets in any lottery/promotion, it makes the SCAM anything but !

The tactics used by the scammers are changing too. Previously winning amount used to be always in millions. Now it seems that they are trying with lower amounts possibly to increase credibility. Some e-mails appear with *official* logos of companies that they claim the lottery was from and photos of actual people as proof. All these could have been lifted from that company's web site without any actual knowledge or involvement of its officers. With the latest web programming technology, some e-mails look so real that even experts may have to make a detailed look before deciphering the traps.

Let us get into it.

< 17 >

Some Basics

The Internet

The *Internet* was probably conceived when Information Technology (IT) was dallying with Telecommunications (T) on a *casual* basis. Later when the Internet was *born*, they paired together and came to be known as IT&T. After realising the potential of their offspring, IT&T formally entered into *wedlock* and came to be known as ICT. Well, it is just my *creative* way of looking at how it all happened. But you get the point that I am making, I am sure.

At the very basic level a network is an interconnection of computer(s) and communication equipment. The Internet is then a network of networks. They are interconnected through network gateways. The whole arrangement works in a distributed fashion allowing every network to *participate* in the information interchange as needed. To make such an exchange of information possible between two components of a network, one or more *protocols* need to be defined. A protocol is an agreed set of terms by which the participants to an information exchange make the task(s) possible reliably. To put it in another way, protocol forms the basis on which software, hardware or both together implement data exchange.

A protocol defines the way a communication objective is achieved. It is typically a list of interconnected tasks, their sequence and the format of exchange(s) to initiate, maintain and conclude data transfer. It typically defines how to interface with other components, what the anticipated exceptions are, how to handle those exceptions when encountered and methods of managing errors in communication that occur from time to time. As the complexity of the functionality that a protocol attempts to specify increases, the complexity of implementing that protocol also increases [6]. This is just a *simplistic* view of things though, meant only as a summary for readers with no or minimal technical background.

< 18 >

The Internet Protocol (IP) defines an *addressing* mechanism by which every *node* within the network identifies itself and others. This is known as the IP address. A group of such nodes form a domain as a single administrative entity. A domain name is a string of characters separated by *dots* and ending in a country specific code except for the USA. A domain name service (DNS) translates a domain name to its corresponding IP address. This allows nodes to communicate with other nodes even in far away domains from anywhere else using network gateways.

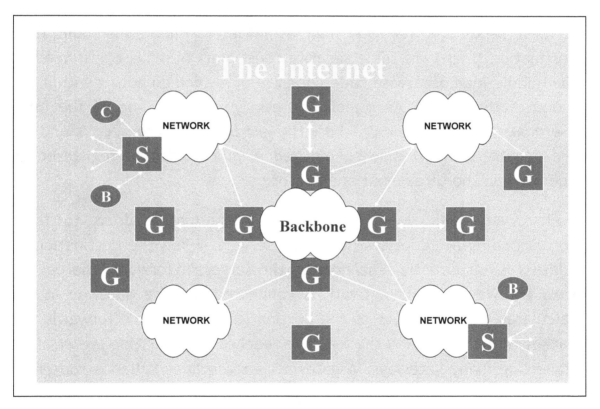

The concept of the Internet started as a research project. However, it was thrown open to the public in the late eighties. Soon business leaders realised its potential to enhance productivity. The concept of Internet Service Provider (ISP) emerged as a business model. Many new tools got developed such as document retrieval systems over the Internet, known as the 'World Wide Web (WWW)'. Old tools such as the Electronic mail – e-mail as it is more popularly known – were adapted to

< 19 >

the new paradigms of the Internet and enabled people to embrace the new technology with enthusiasm and gusto. E-mail is perhaps the most widely used tool for information exchange today using the Internet.

E-mail

E-mail is based on a protocol called *Simple Mail Transfer Protocol* (SMTP). It defines how components on the Internet act as *Mail Transfer Agents* (MTA) to make communication reliable and error free over the net. There are two software components as well, namely a mail-client and a mail-server. As part of the Internet, the mail-server houses the MTA. It sends and receives mail as initiator, middle-man and final destination (there are some security constraints in mails transferred as the middle-man otherwise called *open relay*, which do not fit within the scope of this book). An e-mail address typically will be of the form *username@provider.com.cc* where the last two characters 'cc' stand for the country code. It may be omitted if your domain is registered or operating in the US as mentioned before.

Mail servers map domain names in the e-mail address to their corresponding IP addresses using DNS servers. When the destination IP address is not directly *reachable* by the server, it forwards the packet to a gateway that its network is connected to. The gateway inturn calculates the best *route* to the destination gateway and forwards the packet to it. In this way the message reaches a destination server after traversing many gateways. A gateway is sometimes called a *router* as well.

The mail client resides on the computer of the e-mail user. It periodically interrogates the mail-server for mails addressed to the user(s) and requests to *transfer* mails originating from that computer. The mail-server completes such transactions on the Internet as discussed before. In a web-based e-mail, the client program works as a web application. This can be invoked from any workstation (or any appropriate device) connected to the Internet.

< 20 >

The Service Framework

To acquire Internet connectivity, an individual or a business needs the service of an ISP. In the schematic above the entity 'B' stands for a business and 'C' stands for a non-business client. When a user signs up for service, he/she has to register with an ISP or web based e-mail provider such as hotmail, yahoo, etc. Either the service provider assigns a user-id (that forms part of the e-mail address) or allows the user to choose a unique one. In any case there is a *process* by which the user's *credentials* are *registered* with the provider before a user can use the service. This is called *Authorisation*. The service frame work is depicted below.

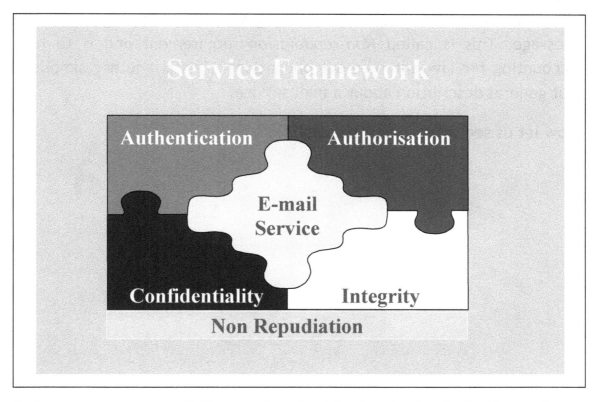

Before a user can avail the service, he/she has to *log in* to the system. This is to ensure that what the user provides as his identification and password at log in match with the credentials that were registered earlier with the provider. This is called *Authentication*. This can be achieved by manually typing those details every time the user logs in or

< 21 >

can be automated through features of the *operating system* that is running on the computer of the user.

The mail system delivers the message only to those explicitly addressed in appropriate fields. *Confidentiality* implies this. *Integrity* implies that the message normally reaches the recipient as sent without any additions or deletions while on transit. However, software *filters* configured at the user's computer may read or scan contents of a mail and it may add 'comments' to the mail as a security feature.

In a header, the mail system records tracking information that any message takes from its origin to destination. The sender and/or receiver will not be able to deny having sent or not having received a message. This is called *Non-repudiation* requirement and is to help accounting for law enforcement obligations. This is another simplistic but general description about a mail service.

Now let us see what constitutes SPAM.

< 22 >

SPAM

History

There are no definite accounts of the word SPAM being an acronym. But I thought that it fitted well with *spurious personally addressed mail*. Its nomenclature is irrelevant though. Any *unsolicited* mail, commercial or personal, may be considered as SPAM. Some people add another word *bulk* to the above to characterise SPAM.

It is said to be a sin for any *engineer* not to have come up with some acronyms in his/her lifetime. So there are unsolicited commercial mail (UCM) and unsolicited bulk mail (UBM), listed under the category of SPAM. I believe I did my bit by trying to portray the word SPAM as an acronym. After all I am an engineer too and I am honour-bound to follow the traditions of my brotherhood. Please excuse me if SPAM *were* indeed an acronym that was coined by another.

SPAM did not originate on the Internet either. It was only adapted to the Internet. Earlier incarnations used to be hand-written and carefully but quietly tucked into someone's school bag or notebook with accounts of a miracle occurred somewhere. It invariably had a religious connection and the victim was asked to spread the news. There used to be tales of rewards for obedience and miseries for not following the instructions. Those were *hoax* chain letters where the perpetrator had to bear the cost of sending.

The same stories were spread on the Internet too in the early 90s using e-mail mainly because prospective victims bear a part of the cost for sending SPAM. The sender could also address multiple recipients at one shot. The most circulated among these probably is a hoax claiming monetary reward from Microsoft for every e-mail sent [7]. This slowly died down at its first appearance but had resurgence again in the late 90s and early 2000s. Stories of bleeding Virgin Mary and milk-drinking idols of Hindu gods and goddesses were all topics in SPAM. But such

< 23 >

religious flavoured mails also slowly gave way to more harmful varieties that we will discuss under SCAMs.

Other variants of SPAM used to be pranks from someone perhaps bored with his/her daily routine and had enough free time to spare. There were fake warnings about viruses tricking you into forwarding those messages to all your contacts. As the stories are often fabricated, the resulting SPAM – though out of good intentions – sometimes caused embarrassment to the sender(s). The deliberate spammers on the other hand claimed that they were only having some fun when caught. However SPAM waste time, use up network bandwidth and clog communication infrastructure costing everyone involved.

A few years ago, I received a chain letter by e-mail with a few of my acquaintances in the chain. I located the initiator's e-mail address at the bottom and responded to him/her (I do not know whether it was a he or a she) but also copying to my contacts in the chain. Assuming that they did not think about the undesirability of SPAM, my intent was only to let them know that it was not good.

Presto ! The spammer shot back an angry e-mail to me with everyone in the chain added to the 'Cc:' filed. The mail contained verbal abuses of every kind. He/she declared to my contacts in the list that I was a hypocrite because I sent SPAM myself by responding to him/her. He/she further accused that I did not like people having some fun. He/she ended the mail with a threat that he/she and his/her contacts would fill my *inbox* with junk mail everyday. Thus I learned my first lesson on SPAM.

Never try to reason with a spammer. It can only make me more vulnerable. The distilled wisdom from that learning may be that one can only reason with another in limited situations.

< 24 >

On those days most e-mail services had limited space allocated (around 2MB) to users; so I was particularly concerned. But then I came across a utility by which I could block specific e-mail addresses from sending me any mail. Well, that saved my day. Nevertheless, some interesting questions may arise from that episode. Was I sending SPAM when it was in response to an e-mail that I received ? You may find *my* answers to such potential questions that you may have at the end of this book under FAQ.

Another SPAM that normally reaches your inbox is from online marketing. You might get a variety of e-mails announcing products and services that you may not be interested. However, it becomes a bit more serious if such mails *inject* any malicious software (*malware*) through attachments or any links provided in it. These things may take place without your knowledge. The more dangerous SPAM types that entice you to losing money are discussed more in detail under e-mail SCAMs.

SPAM Filters

There are a multitude of products offering filtering capabilities to screen e-mail SPAM when they are down-loaded into a user's local computer. Many ISPs and computer operating systems also offer filtering capabilities to their users. Public web based e-mail providers too offer a variety of filtering that is inbuilt with their services. Those filters typically look for some *known* patterns in the content of the mail. If any of them match with known *strings* of characters, then that mail is dropped or tagged as junk mail. The user can then decide whether to really junk it or not.

This has more or less become like the *virus* problems. When protective software becomes available, more and more variants of viruses are injected. Some of them hence escape detection. Similarly not only new variants of SPAM have been introduced but also new techniques have been tried for disguising those specific patterns that are being

< 25 >

automatically checked by software. So the bottom line once again is for the users to be vigilant in deciphering the tricks used by spammer(s).

Types of SPAM

Because of the dearth of information on how SPAM is classified (or at least I have not come across), I venture to do it myself as follows. SPAM that has only nuisance value, I call it junk mail or j-SPAM. But those with a malicious intent behind it, I call it m-SPAM.

Typical varieties of j-SPAM include:

- Chain letters;
  - Hoaxes
  - Pranks
- Announcements;
- Product or Service offers; or
- Other marketing information.

E-mail SCAMs are perfect examples of m-SPAM. Though not always necessarily connected with SPAM directly, readers may also encounter other types of SCAMs such as:

- Web based SCAMs;
- Credit/Debit Card SCAMs
- Telephone SCAMs;
- 'Get Rich Quick' SCAMs.

E-mail seems to be the most used (74%) method in SCAMs for enticing victims in 2006 and 2007 according to the FBI. Web SCAMs accounted for over 30% and telephone SCAMs accounted for 18% during 2007. They were said to be 16.5% and 4.5% respectively in 2005.

< 26 >

An example of j-SPAM follows. This was an unsolicited commercial mail that reached my inbox recently. However, to protect the privacy and respect the confidentiality, I have removed the identities of the recipients and changed the address of the business. As you will see later, some of the patterns in this e-mail resemble that of an m-SPAM. It should alert readers to recognise potential of any vulnerability as well. In any case I believe that it is an example of SPAM whatever its genre one would like to attach it to.

From: sales@somebusinessonline.org [mailto:sales@somebusinessonline.org]
Sent: Sunday, 17 August 2008 2:43 PM
To: <<<removed>>>
Subject: Kind Attention: <<<Removed>>> , An Exclusive Land Investment Offer in and around <<<removed>>>
Importance: High

Dear <<<removed>>> ,

We are introducing the following Real Estate Investment Projects in and around <<<removed>>> from <<<removed>>> per Sq.Ft., These are the Special and the Most Economical Pricing Offered in the Industry by our company. It is being considered the best time to buy real estate now as the prices are likely to shoot up soon. <<<removed>>> currently has got the best prospective opportunities in <<<removed>>> to become the Detroit of <<<removed>>> by its Major Investments like IT, Automobile, Wind Energy by MNC's etc.,

So Never Miss to Invest in the following projects.

Our Projects are as follows:
1. <<<removed>>>

2. <<<removed>>>
....

10. <<<removed>>>

Please Note the above pricing and Offer is valid only until August 31th, 2008, Special Offer for Customers Blocking and Booking the Plots.
....
You may also REFER YOUR FRIENDS and relatives from any part of the World and get benefited from 1% to 2% of the value.

For More Information feel free to contact me,

Warm Regards,
<<<removed>>>

What is in it for them ? Why do they do it ? Perhaps no body will be able to answer such questions completely except a scammer himself/herself. What one can *speculate* though is made possible from various reports of specialist-researchers and crime investigating agencies, and what they

< 27 >

discovered globally. Information collected from victims and the limited investigation reports suggest that one of the objectives of scammer(s) is to steal their victims' identity towards:

o unauthorised withdrawal of money from victims' bank accounts;

o blackmailing victim(s) with demands to pay up money;

o making victim(s) participate in crimes such as money laundering and/or obfuscating the tracks of crimes knowingly or unknowingly.

Scammer(s) could fake your identity with your personal information that they manage to steal and then purchase goods/services or commit crimes in your name. They may also use your details to obtain passports and use them for human trafficking for example; or open bank accounts in your name to take loans, which you may end up paying back. There were *blogs* reporting that in the UK and North America many people have been victims of identity theft. Some have had second mortgages taken out on their first homes without their knowledge. Other reports in the media point to stories of blackmailing.

But you might say: *"Hang on a minute. It all sounds like pure hyperbole to me. You talk about identity theft and the con-artists using my identity to open bank accounts or acquire passports ! It is impossible. To open a bank account you need more than one type of identification of which one should be with an identifiable photo. To get a passport you need a previous passport or a detailed identity check. What you say is pure scaremongering. Don't you think police will catch anyone trying to use a false identity ?"*

You may be absolutely right, but only in an ideal world. Rarely does a criminal get apprehended for identity theft cases because the whole operation is more likely as part of an organised crime. The con-artists seemed to have the know-how and wherewithal to commit such acts, continue their ways and escape from the law. One can find a corrupt law enforcement officer or a bank official or a government officer in most countries who might be working hand-in-glove with such crime syndicates. The scammers were able to open and close bank accounts with absolute ease. Rarely if ever they were caught, they can even turn their victim(s) into scapegoat(s) and make responsible for their crimes. It can at least obfuscate the tracks of the crime for some time and prevent it from leading to the real perpetrators howsoever short that duration may be. Any means to achieve that seemed to be part of their business.

In any case, they wouldn't have booked a vacation to Bahamas and been only waiting for a passport with a handsome/pretty face – i.e., yours – to go with it, would they ? It is unlikely that it is the reason they are after a *scanned copy of your passport* (see examples that follow). Neither would you expect them to pay up your tax liabilities or utility bills on your behalf, would you ? That can not be the reason why they collect your personal information including social security number (SSN). Or would you really believe that the UN has decided to *compensate* fraud-victims (see examples later in this book) globally ? And that you are asked to send your bank details to Nigeria only to collect compensation ?

Let us look at some e-mail SCAMs a bit more closely.

< 29 >

E-mail SCAMs

Organised crimes also operate similar to every *legitimate* business. They have built the required organisational, operational and human infrastructure. Organised crimes too operate with strategies, budgets and objectives. They have their *people, products* and *processes* – the three '*p*'s taught in management courses – like any legitimate corporate business. No wonder they too turned to the Internet and its tools such as e-mails to *grow* their business globally.

Promoters of SCAM are also clever and cunning. As any legitimate business brings new products to market, scammers also bring new variations of their wares to the market. Only vigilant users can thwart their age-old tricks. By spotting questionable or inconsistent patterns in their e-mail offers, we can save ourselves from being deceived.

Patterns of Fraud

According to the dictionary, a SCAM is a scheme for making money by dishonest means. What are the patterns that one should examine in those e-mails then to spot dishonesty ? Typically an e-mail SCAM has the following sections in it.

(a)   An attention-grabber: This is where scammers attempt to attract their victims' attention. It may be an eye-catching announcement of winning large amounts of money, intimation of a breach of security with the recipient's account(s), information about a discount, request for help or advertisement of employment opportunities, etc;

(b)   A story: Then such an e-mail may continue with a story to make the approach look like genuine. It may be just a one-liner or an elaborate gobbledygook. The story section gives a reasonable indication of deception through its contradictions, errors in construction and the like. It is a paradox that even while attempting to deceive, human beings are driven – unknowingly

< 30 >

perhaps – by inherent honesty however little that might be, which leaves something for a discernible observer to expose the dishonesty;

(c)   A direction: Finally, scammers direct their prospective victim(s) to either contact someone by e-mail or phone; or click a link provided within. This may be intended for an initial dialog in which the victim(s) may be given further directions. In some cases the whole e-mail may be just a ruse, because by *opening* its attachment(s) or clicking any link, the recipient's computer could get infected by malware. Invariably the e-mail portrays some urgency to make the recipient act without much thinking. In some other cases, the e-mail ends with a caution to keep the whole content confidential. This is another tell-tale sign of a SCAM in the offing.

The following pages list most varieties of e-mail SCAMs in circulation. A box around some specific word(s) or statements and a number in ordinary brackets following it as a superscript, highlight the patterns. Pointing to those numbers shown as superscripts within the mail, explanatory notes then highlight potential deception, which are given either immediately before or just after those examples. For more avid readers there are a lot of resources listed at the end to horn their skills further. Those sites regularly update more recent sightings.

Types of E-mail SCAMs

The type of e-mail SCAMs could be further divided into Advance Fee Fraud (AFF) and Phishing SCAMs. Similarly phishing SCAMs have been further divided into *simple* phishing and *spear* phishing SCAMs. Most of the examples listed in the following pages fall under the AFF variety but some may also have a *dual* purpose. However, the thrust of this book is not about nomenclature but identifying the patterns in those e-mails as best as one can and hence not to get allured by their claims.

< 31 >

There are numerous possibilities and new versions come up every day very much like computer viruses. However the following variants seem common. They are:

o Announcing banking or credit card problems;

o Online pharmacies;

o Offering freebies including anti-virus and anti-SPAM products;

o Non-existent lottery or promotion prizes;

o Grants/Loans/Inheritances;

o Business proposals/Offers;

o Philanthropy/Charity requests;

o Seeking help to commit fraud;

o Non-existent or unsavoury job offers.

The first three from the above list are examples of phishing SCAMs in general and the rest are variants of the AFF. The AFF type SCAMs are also called the Nigerian or 419 SCAMs. This is because earlier instances of such fraud were traced to Nigeria and the numerals 419 indicate Nigerian legal provision that outlaws such schemes. However, SCAMs of this kind can originate from anywhere these days and may not have anything to do with Nigeria or Nigerians. For a country wise or region wise break-up of the suspected origins of SPAM/SCAM, readers may refer to Wikipedia [3].

There are very 'vanilla' type SCAM mails. There are also those with bells, whistles and all the glitter that scammer(s) could build into 'html' type content. In one e-mail that this Author received, scammer(s) used dynamic text moving from right to left to announce my winning a lottery. Such examples could not be included here due to limitations of static text in a book. However, the patterns are same to what have been listed here without the glitter.

< 32 >

Phishing SCAMs

An unmistakable identity of a Phishing SCAM is that it directs readers to click on a *hyperlink* provided within the mail.

Example 1 – A Banking Fraud

An example of such an e-mail pretending to be from a bank will look like this.

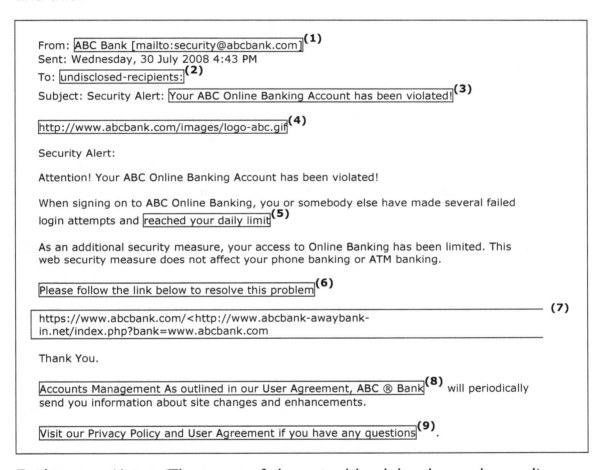

Explanatory Notes (The name of the actual bank has been changed):

1. Typically, an e-mail of this kind will have a display [box (1)] name of the sender like this. This is to give an authentic aura to the mail address. A display name is what one assigns to his/her e-mail address. ISPs do not authenticate any display names to their corresponding e-mail addresses. So, in reality one can put his/her display name to anything to make readers think that the mail is from

< 33 >

a bank, a pharmacy, an online lottery or Buckingham palace or even from the *King/Queen of the universe* if such a person exists. Many examples that follow in later sections will throw further light on this important distinction;

2. This [box (2)] indicates that the same mail has been sent to many recipients. If it were your account/access that was violated, why should it not be addressed to you specifically and only you ?

3. This [box (3)] may be to give a feeling of urgency;

4. The logo [box (4)] may be from a correct link or just copied from the bank's official web site;

5. There are usually no daily limits [box (5)] for log in attempts. For most banks if you or anyone else makes three failed attempts, further access will be temporarily blocked. You need to contact the bank with adequate identification to reset the lock;

6. This [box (6)] is a give away signal that it is a phishing SCAM. If your access to your online banking is limited or locked, you can not and should not resolve it online. You have to identify in person at a branch or by other online identification over the phone;

7. This is a spurious site. When you see 'php?' [box (7)] in the two-line-long link, more than likely it is meant to take you somewhere else that you would regret later;

8. These lines [boxes (8) & (9)] attempt to give an authentic look to the e-mail;

9. If you get an e-mail similar to this as above, it most probably is a phishing SCAM designed to take you to a bogus but look-alike site of a real bank and ask you to enter your personal details there pretending to be for verification.

Lastly, at no time any security conscious bank will send you an *insecure* e-mail in clear text purportedly to resolve a problem. You should always type the URL of the bank or use bookmarks. The browser (unless

< 34 >

infected by malware) uses published DNS entries to find the correct IP address of the bank's official site when you type the URL or use the bookmark. But when you click on a link, the process is *different* and you will reach wherever the scammer(s) wanted you to be.

Example 2 – An Online Pharmacy Fraud

A potential phishing SCAM from an online pharmacy will look like this below. Explanatory notes correspond to the numbers next to the boxes inside:

1. These e-mail addresses could have been spoofed. The address [boxes (1)] points to a telecom service provider in the USA. To protect the identity of the victim [box (2)], it has been removed;

From: jgeorgielm@unidial.com [mailto:jgeorgielm@unidial.com] **(1)**
Sent: Thursday, 21 August 2008 9:01 PM
To: <<<removed>>> **(2)**
Subject: Cheap & discount PrescriptionDrugs, ViagraCailis **(3)** $1.25/Pill, save Your medical bill Up to 80% **(4)** qdu xc

    -= : USA DrugStore : =-
Voted as NO. 1 USA Pharmacy on Internet
Over 85 meds on our online Store
We Accept MasterCard, visa, JCB, Diner and eCheck

You will get a Mystery Gift with Every purchase! **(5)** Limited Time offer!..

Checkout the gift by Clicking below link **(6)**

http://bmt.pqparties.cn **(7)**

2. The address that was there at the 'To:' field seemed to be used as a decoy potentially with multiple addresses in the 'Bcc:' field. A report estimates that such addresses alone in e-mail SCAMs amount to many hundreds of megabytes (MB);

3. These two words [box (3)] without space in between may have been to trick SPAM filter, which may be looking for the word *Viagra* as a *string* to detect pharmacy related SPAM;

4. These [boxes (4) & (5)] are there to entice prospective victim(s);

< 35 >

5. The site [box (7)] identifies a domain in China and was untraceable. Directing to click [box (6)] on a link is a sure-sign identity of a phishing SCAM especially if no such link exists when you type the URL;

6. The link given in the e-mail has no apparent correlation to the sender or the name of the pharmacy that the e-mail cites.

Example 3 – Tricking Anti-SPAM Filters

Here is an e-mail supposedly from another online pharmacy. This is an example of a technique used by scammer(s). By putting their message in a picture, the mail gets past content filters, which normally look for pre-programmed words or phrases in text.

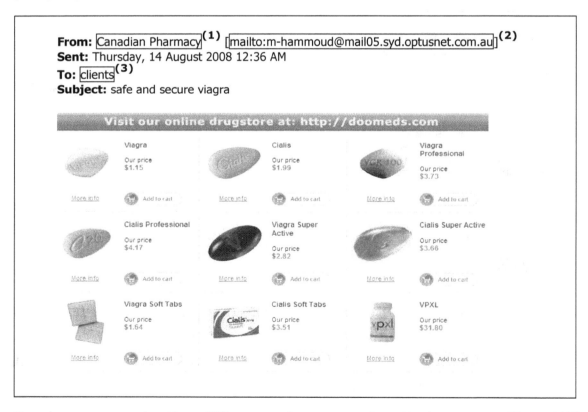

Readers may note the difference between the display name [box (1)] and the return e-mail address used [box (2)]. Also note that the name of the pharmacy in the 'From:' field has no correlation whatsoever to the one in the picture. The site may or may not be from a genuine

< 36 >

online pharmacy but the signs of a SCAM are too good to ignore. One can not be too careful when all sorts of phishing SCAMs exist with similar patterns in this mail. Explanatory Notes (See the corresponding numbers next to the boxes inside):

1. The e-mail [box (2)] either may have been by unauthorised use or spoofed. The e-mail address indicates that it is from an ISP in Australia;

2. It may have been sent to many people [box (3)] with their addresses against the 'Bcc:' field;

3. This does not have a request to click on a link. However, it may have been designed to inject a *worm*, which will do the *phishing* when a recipient opens the e-mail or clicks anywhere on the picture knowingly or by accident.

Example 4 – A Potential Shopping Fraud

This is one of the e-mails that could baffle even a very seasoned user with prior exposure to online SCAMs. Explanatory Notes (The name of the actual business has been changed and a few other words suppressed, varied or omitted):

1. You may note that this appears as a really well-written security alert informing you of a problem with your account [boxes (1), (3), (4), (5), (8), (9), (12), (14) and particularly (15)];

2. You may also give some benefit of doubt that there were probably many others [box (2)] whose accounts have similarly been limited;

3. You may even be concerned that you missed their earlier communication(s) [boxes (6), (7) and (10)] and could straight away fall for the trap;

4. You may perhaps overlook that there has been a repetition of this sentence [box (11)] either by mistake or by intention to stress for effect;

< 37 >

From: Internet Security [mailto:security@ebizonline.com] **(1)**
Sent: Saturday, 30 August 2008 4:43 AM
To: undisclosed-recipients: **(2)**
Subject: Security Alert: Your Online Account has been limited! **(3)**

http://www.ebizonline.com/images/logo-ebiz.gif **(4)**

Dear Member:

Attention! Your account has been limited!

As part of our security measures **(5)**, we regularly screen activity in the ……. system. We recently contacted you after noticing an issue on your account **(6)**. We requested information **(7)** from you for the following reason:

Our system detected unusual charges to a credit card linked to your …… account **(8)**.

Reference Number: ABCD-259-187-991 **(9)**

This is the Last reminder to log in as soon as possible **(10)**. Once you log in, you will be provided with steps to restore your account access. Once you log in, you will be provided with steps to restore your account access **(11)**. We appreciate your understanding as we work to ensure your account safety **(12)**.

Click here to activate your account **(13)**

We thank you for your prompt attention to this matter. Please understand that this is a security measure intended to help protect you and your account **(14)**. We apologise for any inconvenience.

Sincerely,

Protect Your Password: Make sure you never provide your password to fraudulent websites **(15)**.

5. It is more than likely that a victim would have clicked on the link provided. What made me think was that I never registered any details of my credit card or linked it in anyway to this account;

6. Instead of clicking on the link, I contacted the customer service (of the business where I had registered) over telephone just to see whether anyone has *really* used my credit card on this account;

< 38 >

7. That is when I learned that the e-mail was not genuine. The officer told me that there were no credit card transactions with the account but there were a few failed attempts to login.

That means the scammer(s) might have somehow obtained my user-id to that account but could not crack other access requirements including a password. Alternatively, he/she may have my credit card number(s) and wanted to collect other details including a proper mailing address. That would have enabled those con-artists to use my credit/debit card(s) for purchasing goods or services on my account. I continue to get similar e-mails perhaps from different scammers but with the same contents.

< 39 >

Grants/Loans/Inheritances

These AFF type SCAMs could also request personal information that may then be used for identity theft as well.

Example 1 – Queen Elizabeth's Foundation

From: rahman [mailto:rahman@jpa.gov.my] **(1)**
Sent: Friday, 8 August 2008 7:17 PM
To: undisclosed-recipients:
Subject: Attn: Beneficary **(2)** (Contact Mr. Greg Thompson)

From: Queen Elizabeth's Foundation
Woodlands Road, Leatherhead Court
Leatherhead Surrey KT22 0BN.

Attn: Beneficary **(3)**,

PIN NO:QEF/GD/555-2247/2008

Congratulations The Queen Elizabeth's Foundation has chosen you by the board of trustees as one of the final recipients of a cashGrant/Donation for your own personal, educational, and business development. To celebratethe 30th anniversary program, We are giving out a yearly donation of £850,000,00(Eight Hundred And Fifty Thousand Pounds Sterling). to 40lucky recipients, as charity donations/aid from the Queen Elizabeth's Foundation,ECOWAS, EU,UNICEF and the UNO in accordance with the enabling act of Parliament, which is part of our promotion. To file for your claim you are to fill out below information and send it to Mr. Greg Thompson The Executive Secretary Via his email contact address Bellow.

Your Pin Number falls within our United Kingdom Claim office booklet **(4)** and you are directed to contact the Executive Secretary Mr. Greg Thompson in charge of your Donation prize **(5)** / File. Please contact him Via Email /Phone number Bellow immediately.

——————————————————————————————————— **(6)**

Claims Requirements:

1. Full Name:....................................
2. Address:.......................................
3. Nationality:..................................
4. Age:......... Date of Birth:................
5. Occupation:..................................
6. Phone:................Fax:....................
7. State of Origin:..........Country:..............

The Executive Secretary:

Mr. Greg Thompson
Woodlands Road
Leatherhead Court
Leatherhead
Surrey KT22 0BN.
E-mail:greg_thompson222@yahoo.co.uk **(7)**
Tel: +44 702 4046640; FAX:44-44 870 475 3453

Yours Truly,
Mrs.Mary Gray .
Co-ordinator(Queen Elizabeth's Foundation **(8)** cashGrant/Donation).

< 40 >

Explanatory notes:

1. Purported to be from the UK, but this e-mail has an address [box (1)] pointing to a public sector agency in Malaysia;

2. Relatively free from spelling errors except these [boxes (2) & (3)]. May be, scammers too are reading fraud advisories and blogs;

3. This [box (4)] shows that the scammer may have targeted only people from a particular locality;

4. The scammer(s) seem to have left it to recipient(s) to decide whether it was a donation or a prize [box (5)] from the foundation;

5. This is a standard routine [box (6)] in these types of e-mails to seek information like this but dangerous to give them because of a potential for identity theft. Some bloggers report that they responded by filling in such details and are scared to think what could happen next;

6. The contact e-mail address is that from yahoo UK and anyone could obtain such a public e-mail address without much hassle;

7. The foundation [box (8)] whose name and location address figure in this e-mail is a genuine charity *promoting equality for disabled people*. Queen Elizabeth's Hospital Foundation, another charity in Canada, reportedly had a donation/fund-raising drive through a lottery. The scammer(s) may have used both those things very creatively to misguide gullible recipients.

These types of SCAMs offering grants could mutate into others. For example, people seeking financial support for education could fall for an e-mail SCAM pretending to offer scholarships or bursaries.

Example 2 – Foundation de France

Foundation de France is a genuine international body that *helps organisations in Europe and developing nations to realise philanthropic, cultural, scientific and general interest projects*. The

< 41 >

scammer(s) have used the name of a legitimate organisation as in Example 1 above to promote their trade.

Explanatory notes:

1. This looks like a relatively recent version without the mistakes that many advisories and blogs have flagged, making it quite evident that scammers do operate as a business and take feedback seriously;

2. Display name and the sign-off name at the bottom match; however, the e-mail address is a clever adaptation of the foundation's domain name. Instead of 'fdf.org', the e-mail [box (1)] ends with 'frd.org' attempting to fool recipients who did not pay sufficient attention;

3. The address [box (2)] is different to what is there on the official web site of the organisation. However, it seems many variants had arbitrary addresses with some showing addresses even in Italy;

4. This paragraph [box (3)] seems to be clearly lifted from the official site of this organisation to feign some credibility, perhaps;

5. This is an American spelling [box (4)], however could be an error too. Otherwise, it might point to the SCAM originating from somewhere in the North Americas;

6. One can not over-emphasise the potential of identity theft. The details asked for [box (5)] will be sufficient for a skilled scammer to even attempt a remote access on a victim's computer, which in turn can lead to losing whatever banking or personal information stored on it;

7. Finally the prospective victim is being directed to a public e-mail [box (6)] as a usual trick of the trade. Contrast this with the sender's e-mail address at the top, which may even be fake;

8. This [box (7)] is another sure enough pattern to confirm that the e-mail is a SCAM. The scammer(s) do not want recipients to find out this from others;

< 42 >

From: Mr Greg Blenche [mailto:info@frd.org] **(1)**
Sent: Thursday, 7 August 2008 6:03 PM
To: <<<removed>>>
Subject: Foundation De France

Foundation De France
16 Rue Lanterne, Lyon 69001, France. **(2)**
http://www.fdf.org

This email might come to you as a surprise / shock.

The board of trustees of the Foundation de France has given you the privilege to be a beneficiary for the 2008 Cash / Grant Award.

Foundation de France **(3)** was established on the initiative of General De Gaulle and André Malraux in the year 1977 to help individuals and companies to carry out philanthropic, cultural, environmental or scientific projects and social activities. It is a private non-profit organization recognized by the government as a charity working in the public interest. The foundation is an umbrella organization for other foundations; it receives donations and legacies, and awards scholarships and prizes.

After the good work of the Foundation De France, the United Nation decided to contribute, which bring the interest of European Union and the Economic Community of West Africa State. Based on the random selection exercise of internet websites and millions of supermarket cash invoices worldwide,you were selected amongst the lucky recipients to receive the award sum of $1,350,000.00 as charity donations/aid.

(Note that all beneficiaries email addresses were selected randomly from over 100,000 internet websites or a shop's cash invoice around your area in which you might have purchased something from).

You are required to fill the form below and email it to our Executive Secretary below for qualification documentation and processing of your claims. After contacting our office with the requested data, you will be given your donation pin number, which you will used in Claiming the funds.

Please endeavor **(4)** to quote your Qualification number: (FDF-444-6647-9163) in all discussions.

FUND RELEASED AND VERIFICATION FORM
—————————————————————————————————————— **(5)**
1.Full Names:.........
2.Address:.........
3.Sex:.............
4.Age:...............
5.Maritle Status:........
6.Occupation:..........
7.Telephone Number:.......
8.Country:..............
9.Winning ....
10.e-mail address:..........

Executive Secretary - Mr:Greg Blenche Email:executive.secretary05@gmail.com **(6)**

You are by all means hereby advised to keep this whole information confidential **(7)** until you have been able to collect your donation, as there have been many cases of double and unqualified claim, due to beneficiaries informing third parties about his/her donation.

Yours Truly,
Mr Greg Blenche

< 43 >

9. It is only prudent to consult with others when in doubt. There are a lot of resources that put out advisories as listed at the end of this book. As a minimum, readers are urged to do a *Google* search before parting with their hard-earned money or personal details.

Example 3 – Global Savings Loan and Investment

The following is an example for a very short e-mail that is directing its recipient(s) to a public (free) e-mail without much in terms of a story. There was no address in the 'To:' field suggesting that it was sent to many using the 'Bcc:' field. The ISP [box (1)] points to Italy, but as usual it could have been spoofed. The second e-mail address [box (2)], a public e-mail from yahoo, does not necessarily suggest that the scammer(s) may have been or is in the UK.

From: msword_20081 [mailto:msword_20081@libero.it] **(1)**
Sent: Thursday, 24 July 2008 5:29 AM
Subject: Loan Offer Act Fast!!

HELLO
    I AM MR Gary Norman ,THE MANAGING DIRECTOR OF GLOBAL SAVINGS LOAN AND
INVESTMENT .WE GIVE OUT LOANS RANGING FROM BUSINESS
LOANS,INVESTMENTLOANS,MORTGAGE LOANS, AND EQUITY LOANS TO THOSE IN NEED OF IT
AT LOWINTEREST RATE. FOR MORE INFORMATION,CONTACT ME VIA
barr_garynorman@yahoo.co.uk **(2)**

Example 4 – Gareld Financial Company

Yet another short e-mail with signs of an e-mail SCAM. The sender's e-mail address [box (1)] indicates that it belongs to an ISP/portal, a *leading provider of entertainment, information and communications products and service* in the USA. The address against the 'To:' field [box (2)] was removed to protect the privacy of the recipient. This was a public e-mail address that may have been spoofed. The e-mail however has been possibly sent to multiple recipients too.

Usual urgency creator is another [at box (3)] red flag. An unbelievable interest rate [box (4)] unfortunately appeals to people who are really in need of some financial support. Standard patterns of errors [boxes (5), (6) & (7)] are other indicators of a SCAM. At the end the sender invites

< 44 >

the recipient(s) to use another e-mail address [box (8)] and that is from one of the Microsoft portals. Also the sender might have forgotten to include a form [box (7)] as in earlier cases. The e-mail below does not appear to be a genuine marketing e-mail, in any case.

From: gareldloanfirm@comcast.net [mailto:gareldloanfirm@comcast.net] **(1)**
Sent: Thursday, 24 July 2008 3:17 AM
To: <<<removed>>> **(2)**
Subject: HURRY NOW FOR AN EASY PAY LOAN HERE TODAY **(3)**

Hello,
To July 2008 success subscribers, I Mr Gareld Emerson the director of Gareld financial Company is inviting all interested loan seekers to kindly apply for their requested amount here in gareldloaninvestment@live.com My lending rate is 3% **(4)** and with the lenth **(5)** of one to ten years(1-10yrs)
All interested applicant are advice **(6)** to fill the below form **(7)** and forward to us his/her e-mail to gareldloaninvestment@live.com **(8)**

Your mail will be kindly attended to soonest after your Mailback.
Regards

Example 5 – An ATM Card Offer

Explanatory notes:

1. One may be amazed by the creativity of these scammers whoever they are to have come up with such unbelievable stories [boxes (4), (5), (6) & (7)];

2. The display name [box (1)] and the sender's return e-mail address [box (2)] seem specifically created for this purpose. The domain [box (2)] points to a Spanish Internet portal. A Nigerian SCAM with a Spanish flavour ?

3. Incidentally, most AFF SCAMs come with e-mail contents written in all capitals;

4. This e-mail was directly addressed to the recipient [box (3)] showing that the scammers used a legitimate e-mail address, wherever they got it from. This address has been removed to protect the privacy of the recipient;

< 45 >

From: ATM CARD PAYMENT FOR FUND BENEFICIARIES **(1)**
[atmbeneficia@hispavista.com] **(2)**
Sent: Friday, 15 August 2008 2:56 AM
To: <<<Removed>>> **(3)**
Subject: ATM CARD PAYMENT FOR FUND BENEFICIARIES

OFFICE OF THE SENATE HOUSE, FEDERAL REPUBLIC OF NIGERIA
COMMITTEE ON FOREIGN PAYMENT (RESOLUTION PANEL ON CONTRACT/INHERITANCE PAYMENT) IKOYI-LAGOS NIGERIA

ATM CARD PAYMENT FOR FUND BENEFICIARIES INTERNATIONAL CREDIT SETTLEMENT OFFICE OF THE DIRECTOR OF OPERATIONS, G.T.BANK OF NIGERIA.

ATTENTION BENEFICIARY:

(4)
THIS IS TO OFFICIALLY INFORM YOU THAT WE HAVE VERIFIED YOUR CONTRACT /INHERITANCE FILE AND FOUND OUT THAT WHY YOU HAVE NOT RECEIVED YOUR PAYMENT IS BECAUSE YOU HAVE NOT FULFILLED THE OBLIGATIONS GIVEN TO YOU IN RESPECT OF YOUR CONTRACT / INHERITANCE PAYMENT.

SECONDLY WE HAVE BEEN INFORMED THAT YOU ARE STILL DEALING WITH THE NONE OFFICIALS IN THE BANK ALL YOUR ATTEMPT TO SECURE THE RELEASE OF THE FUND TO YOU. WE WISH TO ADVICE YOU THAT SUCH AN ILLEGAL ACT LIKE THIS HAVE TO STOP IF YOU WISHES TO RECEIVE YOUR PAYMENT SINCE WE HAVE DECIDED TO BRING A SOLUTION TO YOUR PROBLEM. **(5)** RIGHT NOW WE HAVE ARRANGED YOUR PAYMENT THROUGH OUR SWIFT CARD PAYMENT CENTER ASIA PACIFIC, THAT IS THE LATEST INSTRUCTION BY THE PRESIDENT ALHAJI UMARU YAR'ADUA WHO WAS ELECTED IN ON THE 29TH MAY 2007 (GCFR) FEDERAL REPUBLIC OF NIGERIA. **(6)** THIS CARD CENTER WILL SEND YOU AN ATM CARD WHICH YOU WILL USE TO WITHDRAW YOUR MONEY IN ANY ATM MACHINE IN ANY PART OF THE WORLD, BUT THE MAXIMUM IS TWO THOUSAND FIVE HUNDRED DOLLARS PER DAY, SO IF YOU LIKE TO RECEIVE YOUR FUND THIS WAY PLEASE LET US KNOW BY CONTACTING THE CARD PAYMENT CENTER AND ALSO SEND THE FOLLOWING INFORMATION: **(7)**

1.YOUR FULL NAME; 2. PHONE AND FAX NUMBER; 3. ADDRESS WERE YOU WANT THEM TO SEND THE ATM CARD **(8)**; 4. YOUR AGE AND CURRENT OCCUPATION; 5. A COPY OF YOUR IDENTITY ATTACHED TO E-MAIL **(9)**; 6,AND YOUR BANKING INFORMATION CONTACT PERSON **(10)**:

MR LAWSON KOLAPO INTEGRATED PAYMENT DEPARTMENT
EMAIL, kolapomrlawson2@yahoo.com **(11)** TELE PHONE +234-80-56088954

THE ATM CARD PAYMENT CENTER HAS BEEN MANDATED TO ISSUE OUT $8,300,000.00 AS PART PAYMENT FOR THIS FISCAL YEAR 2008. WHICH YOU ARE ADVICE TO CONTACT NOW THAT THE NEW ELECTED PRESIDENT HAS TAKEN OVER THE GOVERNMENT FOR THE RELEASE OF YOUR FUND, ALSO FOR YOUR INFORMATION YOU HAVE TO STOP ANY FURTHER COMMUNICATION WITH ANY OTHER PERSON(S) OR OFFICE(s) **(12)**. THIS IS TO AVOID ANY HITCHES IN FINALIZING YOUR PAYMENT. CALL ME ON MY DIRECT NUMBER +234-80-32635403 IN THIS REGARDS AND ALSO UPDATE ME ON ANY DEVELOPMENT **(13)** FROM THE ABOVE MENTIONED OFFICE.

NOTE:

(14)
THAT BECAUSE OF IMPOSTORS, WE HEREBY ISSUED YOU OUR CODE OF CONDUCT, WHICH IS (118) SO YOU HAVE TO INDICATE THIS CODE WHEN CONTACTING THE CARD CENTER.

< 46 >

5. Your address [box (8)], a copy of any identity [box (9)] and contact person for your banking information [box (10)] are some of the things that one should never send over unsecure e-mail in any case;

6. You are asked to contact a free e-mail address from yahoo [box (11)]. Contrast this with the sender's address [box (2)] on top;

7. As usual for a SCAM of this type you are asked to keep it confidential [boxes (12)]. Perhaps to make it appear legitimate, you are given a direct phone number to the sender [box (13)] too and a code (?) of conduct [box (14)] whatever that means;

There were some more lines as a sign-off with the same information at the top and telephone numbers. They were removed to make those parts that are more relevant, fit on a single page.

Example 8 – A Kind Uncle

Explanatory notes:

1. The address [box (1)] used to send this mail seems to be a legitimate address of someone from 'Metric Construction Corporation', a construction management services provider headquartered in Boston. It may have been by unauthorised access or spoofed;

2. The mail does not seem to have any entry against 'To:' field. Yet it is possible that, the mail has been sent to many using 'Bcc:' field;

3. As usual the contact e-mail address [boxes (2) & (6)] is different from the one used to send the mail;

4. Well, the story [box (3)] may be credible to many, especially seeing an apparent failed attempt [box (4)] to notify them earlier. But do they not spell the word [box (5)] differently in the UK ?

5. If you did fall for it, the scammer does not seem to want you to know the truth from anyone else either [box (7)] as usual.

< 47 >

From: Bob Puracchio [mailto:bpuracchio@metriccorp.com] **(1)**
Sent: Tuesday, 29 July 2008 8:14 PM
Subject: Response!!!!!

Barristers' Chambers:.. THE WILL HAVE BEEN EXECUTED
KINSLEY WOODS & ASSOCIATES
Phone: +44 703 194 7253; Fax: +44 700 592 1653

E-mail: kinsleywoods@yahoo.com **(2)**
Address:33 Bedford Row
London WC1R 4JH, England
DAVID SINGER & ASSOCIATES LONDON - UK.

Attention:

_____ **(3)**

On behalf of the Trustees and Executor of the estate of Late Engr. Jurgen Krugger. I once again try to notify you as my earlier letter was returned undelivered **(4)**. I hereby attempt to reach you again by this same email address on the WILL. I wish to notify you that late Jurge Krugger made you a beneficiary in his WILL. He left the sum of Thirty Million, One Hundred Thousand Dollars (USD$30, 100.000.00) to you in the Codicil and last testament to his WILL. This may sound strange and unbelievable to you, but it is real and true. Being a widely travelled man, he said he met you sometime in the past or simply you were nominated to him by one of his numerous friends abroad who wished you good, I am not too sure again. Jurgen Krugger until his death was a member of the Helicopter Society and the Institute of Electronic & Electrical Engineers and a German property magnate. He was a very dedicated christian who loved to give out alms to the poor,hungry and needy. His great philanthropy earned him numerous awards during his life time. Late Jurgen Krugger died on the 13th day of December, 2004 at the age of 80 years, and his WILL is now ready for execution after 3 years and thorough investigations. According to him, this money is to support your humanitarian/medical activities and to help the poor and the needy in our society. Please if I reach you as I am hopeful, endeavor **(5)** to get back to me as soon as possible to enable me conclude my job. I hope to hear from you in no distant time.

Note: You are advised to contact me with my personal email address below:

E-mail: kinsleywoods@yahoo.com **(6)** Phone: +44 703 194 7253

I await your prompt response and please keep this very discrete and to yourself until the transfer of the funds to you is finalised **(7)**.

Yours in Service,
BARRISTER KINSLEY WOODS
PRINCIPAL PARTNERS
PARTNERS: Barrister Aidan Walsh, Markus Wolfgang, Mr. John Marvey Esq, Mr. Jerry Smith Esq

Example 9 – A Benevolent Aunt

Explanatory notes:

1. As in example 8 above, the address used to send this mail [box (1)] may have been either spoofed or by unauthorised access. The address points to an organisation producing digital artwork, named Virgil Visions. However, the same display name 'Mrs. Virgil H. Storrs'

< 48 >

appears in another e-mail SCAM listed under 'You have a package' later in this book (see page 78);

From: Mrs. Virgil H. Storrs [mailto:info@virgil.com] **(1)**
Sent: Wednesday, 23 July 2008 6:22 PM
To: undisclosed-recipients **(2)**
Subject: Greetings !!

Greetings!

(3)

I have been waiting for you since to contact me for your Confirmable BankDraft of $1,000.000.00 United States Dollars,but I did not hear from you since that time. Then I went and deposited the Draft with FedEx COURIER SERVICE,West Africa,I travelled out of the country for a 3 Months Course and I will not come back till end of July.

What you have to do now is to contact the FedEx COURIER SERVICE as soon as possible (4) to know when they will deliver your package to you because of the expiring date **(4)** .For your information, I have paid for the delivering Charge,Insurance premium and Clearance Certificate Fee of the Cheque showing that it is not a Drug Money or meant to sponsor Terrorist attackin your Country **(5)** . The only money you will send to the FedEx COURIER SERVICE **(6)** to deliver your Draft direct to your postal Address in your country is $100 USD)only being Security Keeping Fee **(7)** of the Courier Company so far.Again,don't be deceived by anybody **(8)** to pay any other money except$100 USDDollars you are to pay the Security Keeping Fee **(9)** .

I would have paid **(10)** that but they said no because they don't know when you will contact them and in case of demurrage **(11)** . You have to contact the FedEx COURIER SERVICE now for the delivery of your Draft with this information bellow;

=====Customer Care Unit===

Contact Person: Kenneth Cole; Email Address: fedexngria@gmail.com **(12)**
Telephone: +234 8066956344
===
Finally, make sure that you reconfirm your Postal address; Direct telephone number **(13)** ;
Do send it to them again to avoid any mistake on the Delivery **(14)** and ask them to give you the tracking number to enable you track your package over there and know when it will get to your address.

Yours Faithfully,

2. The e-mail seems to have been sent to multiple recipients [box (2)];

3. The story may be true but only under a *willing suspension of disbelief* [boxes (3) to (11), (13) and (14)] that one can accept it, particularly as this kind lady went all the way from the USA to West Africa to send the draft by 'FedEx';

< 49 >

4. Well, you may already know that FedEx has its own e-mail addresses and does not have to sign up with *gmail* [box (12)], a free e-mail service from Google.

5. You may want to compare these aforementioned patterns with other examples as well.

< 50 >

Lottery SCAMs

There have been many variants of non-existing lotteries in circulation as listed here. Readers may find many more too from the resources listed at the end of this book.

Example 1 – Irish Lottery

From: IRISH LOTTERY [info@irmail.net] (1)
Sent: Wednesday, 27 August 2008 8:52 PM
Subject: Claims Notification!!!

The Irish Lottery
P O Box 1010
11 G Lower Dorset Street, Dublin 1, Ireland
(Customer Services)
Ref: UK/9420X1/64 Batch: 077/07/ZY369

WINNING NOTIFICATION:

(2)
You have been Selected on the Irish Lottery Draw Held on Saturday, Wed 04 Jun 2008 - 7:57pm, Our lottery program selection has finally been performed today which was held at the Marina office. IRISH Promotion is a joint Euro/America private lottery registered and organized (3) in accordance with the World Lottery Regulation act. We the National Lottery organizing (4) committee are pleased to officially notify you of the status of your email application (5).

An official notification of winning is hereby issued to you as your email promotion ticket randomly drew for the Lucky Numbers: 04 Jun 2008 -,04, 11, 17,33, 40, 42, - Bonus 02, which selected your email as the 1ST winner of our lottery program you have consequently won the lottery program in the first batch.Suffice to say here, We have officially approved a sum payout of €9,000,000 Euro (€9 Million Euro.) to you as the lottery winner.

You are hereby required to contact your FIDUCIARY AGENT (6) with below details for your winning funds.

Mr Bill Karl
Tel: +44 7031 9558 87; +44 7031 9484 87
Email: mail@fidkarl.vossnet.co.uk (7)
       fid_karl@yahoo.com.hk (8)

(9)
VERIFICATION AND FUNDS RELEASE FORM
FULL NAMES: AGE: SEX: ADDRESS: COUNTRY: MARITAL STATUS: OCCUPATION: PHONE NUMBER: FAX NUMBER:

Congratulations from all our staff for being part of IRISH 2008 LOTTERY PROGRAM (10).

Yours faithfully,
Meg Stone (Mrs.)
Online coordinator for THE IRISH LOTTERY

< 51 >

Explanatory notes:

1. As typical of these type of e-mails, you have a winning notification [box (2)] with a story of a lottery that you never registered with, but still asking you to contact an agent [box (6)] to claim your prize;

2. For a notification from Ireland with reference to the UK, US spellings [boxes (3) & (4)] are used. This should further indicate that this is a fraudulent e-mail especially when you have not applied [box (5)] or registered your name for any lottery;

3. There are two e-mail addresses [boxes (7) & (8)] for a change. The first has been widely publicised on the web as part of an advisory on fraud and that might be why another was added;

4. The information sought [box (9)] is minimum compared to others, yet one should not be carried away by that. If you made a quick Google search on these [boxes (1) & (10)], you may realise that this is a SCAM without any further analysis.

Example 2 – Yahoo Awards Lottery

Explanatory notes:

1. By now readers may have become familiar with the patterns to be watched out. Nevertheless, some of the more obvious signs have been identified again in this example;

2. As mentioned earlier, a quick search on the Internet will confirm that this is an e-mail SCAM too. It was perhaps easy for the scammer to use his free e-mail from yahoo [box (1)] to make his/her claim look real to some recipients;

3. There seems to be multiple recipients [box (2)] as usual to these types of SCAMs;

4. A story as usual too [box (3)] but gone are the days when the winnings were invariably multi-million dollars, pounds or Euros as in earlier SCAMs;

< 52 >

From: YAHOO AWARDS LOTTERY 2008 [winningnotification@yahoo.com] **(1)**
Sent: Sunday, 24 August 2008 9:54 PM
To: undisclosed-recipients : **(2)**
Subject: ***CONGRATULATION YOU HAVE WON****

Yahoo Awards Center
124 Stockport Road,
Longsight, Manchester M60 2DB - United Kingdom

(3)
This is to inform you that you have won a prize money of TWO HUNDRED AND FIFTY THOUSAND POUNDS Great Britain Pounds (250,000.00) for the 2008 Promotion which is Organized by YAHOO AWARDS & WINDOWS LIVE. YAHOO! collects all the email addresses of the people that are active online, among the millions that subscribed to Yahoo and Hotmail and few from other e-mail providers. Six people are selected monthly to benefit from this promotion and you are one of the Selected Winners.

PAYMENT OF PRIZE AND CLAIM

Winners shall be paid in accordance with his/her Settlement Centre. Yahoo Prize Award must be claimed not later than 15 days from date of Draw Notification **(4)**. Any prize not claimed within this period will be forfeited **(5)**. These numbers fall within the England Location file and you are requested to contact our fiduciary agent in Manchester **(6)** and send your winning filled form below to him;

Agent Name: Dr.Kevin James
E-Mail: department_claims_2008@live.com **(7)** Tel: +447045757412

(8)
****
PRIZE AWARD VERIFICATION FORM PERSONAL DETAILS:
NAME   (MR.   MRS.MS.):................................   FULL   ADDRESS
:.......................... DIRECT   MOBILE   TEL :.............................. EMAIL
ADDRESS :...................................... OCCUPATION:...
MARITAL   STATUS:.....................................   DATE   OF
BIRTH:.. COUNTRY...
PRIZE WINNING DETAILS: BATCH#:.YPA/06/APA-43658 REF.#:.. 2008234522
WINNING#....1206 AMOUNT WON. 250,000.00.
****

(9)
NOTE: THIS VERIFICATION FORM SHOULD BE COMPLETELY FILLED OUT AND RETURN
TO THIS EMAIL (department_claims_2008@live.com)
Dr Kevin James Phone Number: +447045757412

AGENT EMAIL: department_claims_2008@live.com

As soon as our agent hears from you, he shall commence the process that will facilitate the release of your fund to you. Congratulations!! once again.

Yours in service,
Dr. (Mrs.) Edith Barth

WARNING! Do not tell people about your Prize Award **(10)** until your money is successfully handed over to you to avoid disqualification that may arise from double claim. You may also receive similar e-mails from people potraying **(11)** to be other Organizations or Yahoo Inc.

(12)
This is solely to collect your personal information from you and lay claim over your winning. In event that you receive any e-mail similar to the notification letter that was sent to you, Kindly delete it from your mail box and give no further correspondence to such person or body

< 53 >

5. Another way of hurrying you [box (4) & (5)] to contact their agent making you think that any delay will make you lose your fortune;

6. If you are wondering [box (6)] whether you were eligible if you are not residing in the locality mentioned, be reminded that the whole story is fake any way;

7. Readers may have also realised the irony that the contact e-mail address provided [box (7)] is a free-to-join variety from Microsoft and different to the one from yahoo used before [box (1)];

8. The scammer(s) seem to have improved their presentation as there are only three errors [see boxes (9), (11) & (12)] that I could spot;

9. A confidentiality clause [box (10)] is there as well. However, it may appear that there is stiff competition [box (12)] in the SCAM business too.

Example 3 – UK National Lottery

Explanatory notes:

1. The display name [box (1)] may not have anything to do with the e-mail address used [box (2)] to send this e-mail. This e-mail address points to an ISP in Australia. Reading in light of what is given at the end [box (10)], it is more likely that this is an example of unauthorised usage of the e-mail by another;

2. Boxes (3), (4) (5) & (9) provide those usual ingredients to such e-mails;

3. There are two contact e-mail addresses [boxes (6) & (7)] in this example as well, but the second is more likely an undeliverable address or a decoy to inject malicious software if clicked;

4. I could only spot one error [box (8)] in this and hence the mail may have been constructed by a native speaker or a well-educated person with good English proficiency.

< 54 >

```
From: UK NATIONAL LOTTERY (1) [rphelps@aapt.net.au] (2)
Sent: Wednesday, 23 July 2008 10:28 PM
To: undisclosed-recipients (3) :
Subject: CONGRATULATION YOU HAVE WON (CONTACT FOR VERIFICATION)

Dear Winner,
```
(4)
This is to notify you that you have won £850,000.00 (Eight hundred and fifty Thousand Pounds Sterling) in our online email lottery Draw in which e-mail addresses are picked randomly by computerised balloting, powered by the Internet. Ticket no: 56475600545 188

To claim your prize, please contact: Fiduciary Agent Mr Barret Johnson (5)
Tell: +44 703 196 2680
Tell: +44 703 196 1795
Email: fiduciaryclaimsdept@hotmail.co.uk (6)
Email: info_barretjohnsondept@lotteryclaims.co.uk (7)
With the following information's (8)

(9)
```
=================================================================
VERIFICATION FORM
FULL NAMES
ADDRESS:
OCCUPATION:
COUNTRY:
AGE, SEX:
TELEPHONE
=================================================================
Yours Truly,
David TERMAN (Mr) Co-Coordinator (On-line Promo Programme).
```
(10)
Please note that this is an automated message. Do not click your reply button. Send details to contact e-mail above.

Example 4 – British Online Lottery

Explanatory notes:

1. The e-mail address used to send this mail [box (1)] seems to be forged. The domain could not be traced. The display name is fake and there is no British Online (international) Lottery either [box(9)];

2. Other usual patterns include, multiple recipients [box (2)], errors [boxes (3) & (5)], a contact officer [box (6)], a public e-mail contact [box (7)] and asking you to furnish details [box (8)];

3. If all those providers joined together [box (4)] and chose your personal e-mail, you are still asked to provide your e-mail address once again [box (8), item 9];

< 55 >

4. Readers may want to compare the patterns in this e-mail with other e-mail SCAMs;

5. Perhaps to try and make you convinced of the legitimacy of the story, a clause for disqualification [box (10)] too !

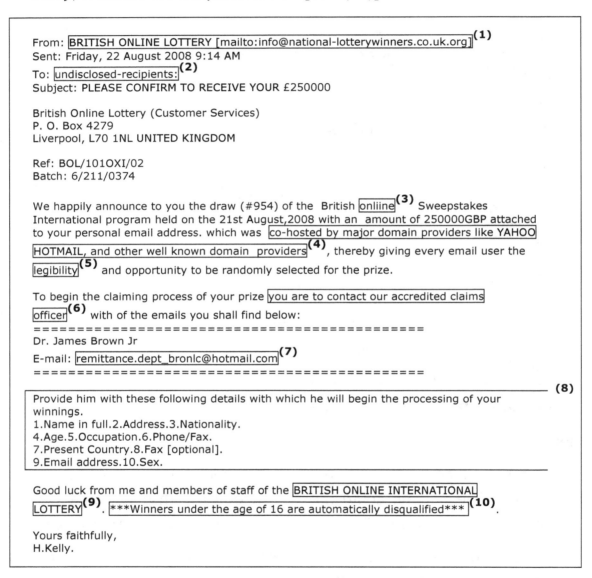

From: BRITISH ONLINE LOTTERY [mailto:info@national-lotterywinners.co.uk.org] (1)
Sent: Friday, 22 August 2008 9:14 AM
To: undisclosed-recipients: (2)
Subject: PLEASE CONFIRM TO RECEIVE YOUR £250000

British Online Lottery (Customer Services)
P. O. Box 4279
Liverpool, L70 1NL UNITED KINGDOM

Ref: BOL/101OXI/02
Batch: 6/211/0374

We happily announce to you the draw (#954) of the British onliine (3) Sweepstakes International program held on the 21st August,2008 with an amount of 250000GBP attached to your personal email address. which was co-hosted by major domain providers like YAHOO HOTMAIL, and other well known domain providers (4), thereby giving every email user the legibility (5) and opportunity to be randomly selected for the prize.

To begin the claiming process of your prize you are to contact our accredited claims officer (6) with of the emails you shall find below:
===
Dr. James Brown Jr

E-mail: remittance.dept_bronlc@hotmail.com (7)
===
_____ (8)
Provide him with these following details with which he will begin the processing of your winnings.
1.Name in full.2.Address.3.Nationality.
4.Age.5.Occupation.6.Phone/Fax.
7.Present Country.8.Fax [optional].
9.Email address.10.Sex.
_____

Good luck from me and members of staff of the BRITISH ONLINE INTERNATIONAL LOTTERY (9). ***Winners under the age of 16 are automatically disqualified*** (10).

Yours faithfully,
H.Kelly.

Example 5 – UK Lottery Organization

Explanatory notes:

1. The e-mail address [box (1)] looks like it was generated by some computer software;

< 56 >

2. This was directed to a specific recipient address and hence it has been removed. However, the mail could still have been sent to multiple recipients with their addresses in the 'Bcc:' field;

3. I am not sure whether the Japanese (or is it Chinese ?) text [box (3)] is a translation for the story [box (4)];

4. However, this e-mail has most of the ingredients to make it an indisputable candidate for an e-mail SCAM;

5. Incidentally, there is no UK Lottery Organization [box (5)]. Also note the American spelling.

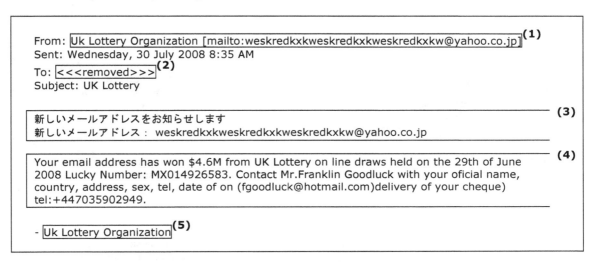

From: Uk Lottery Organization [mailto:weskredkxkweskredkxkweskredkxkw@yahoo.co.jp] (1)
Sent: Wednesday, 30 July 2008 8:35 AM
To: <<<removed>>> (2)
Subject: UK Lottery

新しいメールアドレスをお知らせします (3)
新しいメールアドレス： weskredkxkweskredkxkweskredkxkw@yahoo.co.jp

Your email address has won $4.6M from UK Lottery on line draws held on the 29th of June (4)
2008 Lucky Number: MX014926583. Contact Mr.Franklin Goodluck with your oficial name,
country, address, sex, tel, date of on (fgoodluck@hotmail.com)delivery of your cheque)
tel:+447035902949.

- Uk Lottery Organization (5)

Example 6 – Microsoft Mega Jackpot Lottery

Explanatory notes:

1. There are many variants of non-existent lotteries purported to be from Microsoft alone;

2. The e-mail address [box (1)] used to send this mail points to 'Crnogorski Telekom' in Montenegro but may have been spoofed or by unauthorised usage;

3. This e-mail did not have a 'To:' field indicating that multiple recipients might have received the e-mail, their addresses being in the 'Bcc:' field;

< 57 >

From: MICROSOFT LOTTERY [alfacg@t-com.me] **(1)**
Sent: Thursday, 24 July 2008 10:05 AM
Subject: CONTACT YOUR CLAIMS AGENT??? **(2)**

Importance: High

20 Craven Park,
Harlesden London NW10, United Kingdom
Batch: BTD/734/07 Ref:MSW/56B-672GH/L

MICROSOFT MEGA JACKPOT LOTTERY PROMOTIONS, EMAIL AWARD PROMO:

(3)

Finally today, we announce the winners of the MICROSOFT MEGA JACKPOT LOTTOWINNINGS PROGRAMS , Your company or your personal e-mail address, attached to winning number 23-76-06-54-42-100, with serial number647489, consequently won in the Tenth lottery category.
You are therefore been approved for lump sums pay out of GBP 1.000.000 POUNDS ($2.000.000 USD) in cash Credited to file REF NO:MSW/56B-672GH/L and winning number 23-76-06-54-42-100, this is from total prize money of GBP 25.000.000 POUNDS, shared among the Twenty five (25)international winners in this category.

All participants were selected through our Microsoft computer ballot system drawn form 42,000 Names, 6,000 names from each continent, as part of International E-MAIL Promotions Program, for our prominent MS WORD user all over the world, and for the Continuous use of E-mail.
 Your fund (certified Cashiers c heque) has been insured with your REF NO: MSW/56B-672GH/L and winning number 23-76-06-54-42-100.

To claim your winning prize, you must first contact the claims department by email **(4)** for Processing and remittance of your prize money to you. The claims processor is:

Name:Daves Adams
Email.davesadams11@live.com **(5)**

Do email the above email a ddresses, all at once. In order to avoid unnecessary delays and complications, please remember to quote your reference and winning numbers in all correspondences with your claims officer.

(6)

PLEASE NOTE THAT YOU ARE TO SEND THE BELOW INFORMATIONS REQUIRED TO CLAIM YOUR WINNING PRIZE:
1. Full Name: ....
2. Address: ....
3. Nationality: ....
4. Age: ....Date of Birth: ......
5. Occupation: ....
6. Phone: ....Fax: ....
7. State of Origin: ....Country: ....
8: DELIVERY OPTIONS

DELIVERY OPTIONS:
(1): BANK SWIFT WIRE TRANSFER **(7)**
(2): COME TO OUR OFFSHORE PAYMENT CENTER IN UK **(8)**
(3): BY OUR COURIER FIRM, **(9)**

Sincerely,
Mrs. Maurrine Diane H.
Secretary

< 58 >

4. Apart from all other normal patterns [boxes (2), (3), (4), (5) & (6)], this e-mail seems to have an innovation of giving options [boxes (7), (8) & (9)] to prospective victim(s) towards collecting their winning amount;

5. The first option [box (7)] is to collect bank details, which could invariably lead to wiping out the whole balance in their accounts;

6. The third option [box (9)] will collect money under various categories (see other examples such as 'A benevolent Aunt' and 'You have a Packet') from victim(s);

7. The second option may have been intended to instil a level of credibility but seems to be the most dangerous option. According to US State Department reports quoted on a web site (see Resources listed at the end) as a warning, it appears that victims could be *beaten, subjected to threats and extortion, and in some cases, even murdered*;

8. That should serve as an eye-opener against this option [box (8)] for anyone who is not convinced enough still;

9. Finally, *"We're sorry to say that you did not win the Microsoft Lottery, because there is no Microsoft Lottery"*, said a Microsoft spokesperson on an official blog site from the company.

Example 7 – National Sports Lottery

Explanatory notes:

1. The National Sports Lottery plc is registered in Nigeria and the e-mail address [box (1)] used to send this e-mail points to an ISP in Chile;

2. Readers may make a special note of the three different e-mail addresses listed in this mail [boxes (1), (12) & (15)] and the fact that they do not in any way relate to the organisation;

3. The 'British Gambling Board' [box (4)] may have been a clever adaptation of 'The Gaming Board for Great Britain';

< 59 >

From: The National Sports Lottery plc [mailto:leonor.pino@tie.cl] (1)
Sent: Tuesday, 19 August 2008 9:43 AM
Subject: NSL Winning Notification Of (500,000.00 GBP) (2)

(3)

The National Sports Lottery plc
National Sports Lottery.
No22 Wema Road,Lagos, Nigeria,
West Africa

This is to inform you that you have been selected for a cash prize of 500,000 GBP (Five Hundred Thousand Great British Pounds) This selection process was carried out through random selection in our computerized email selection system (ESS) from a database of over 5,000 e-mail addresses drawn from which you were selected.

The NSL AWARD DEPARTMENT, is approved by the British Gambling Board (4), due to this slection (5) Your email address as indicated was drawn and attached to ticket NO: 00190 Ref NSL100208 with the lucky No:14-21-25-39-40-47(20) which subsequently won you 500,000.GBP (Five Hundred Thousand Great British Pounds), A winning cheque has been issued in your name by (NSL AWARD DEPARTMENT CO_OPERATION BOARD) and also a certificate of prize claims will be sent along side with your winnings cheque to you. You are therefore expected to contact (6) (Sky Net Courier Service) with the following information stated below.

(7)

Provide them with the information below:

1.Full Name:_____
2.Full Address:_____
3.Marital Status:_____
4.Occupation:_____
5.Age:_____
6.Sex:_____
7.Nationality:_____
8.Country Of Residence:_____
9.Telephone Number:_____
10.Ref Number:_____
11.Amount Wom (8):_____

NB: State mean (9) to collect this winnings.

1: Sky Net Courier Delivery :................ (Yes or No) (10)
2: Bank Transfer :................................. (Yes or No) (11)

SKY NET COURIER SERVICE
Mr. Willans Nath (DES-PATCH OFFICER)
Email : skynet-delivery@live.com (12)
Telephone No: +2348050266840.

Congratulations once more from members and staff of this program.

Sincerely,
National Sport (13) Lottery (A Passion for Change Lives (14))
Mr Uwadiae Bello.
NSL Pulice Related Agent.
Email: mr_uwadiaebello@hotmail.com (15)

< 60 >

4. This e-mail also contains those usual patterns of fraud including a story [box (3)], a few errors [boxes (5), (8), (9), (13) & (14)], asking you to contact someone [box (5)], a form to fill in [box (7)], etc., as identified in examples before;

5. Two of the e-mails [boxes (12) & (15)] are free-to-join e-mail services from Microsoft. The other e-mal address [box (1)] figures in another example too (see 'Run this Charity', page 66);

6. One blogger had stated that he called the scammer from a public phone and told them to get a real job. It may be very tempting to show outrage but it may be far more prudent to leave the task of 'educating' scammer(s) to the appropriate authorities.

< 61 >

Promotion Prizes

Example 1 – Shell Lottery International Online Promotion

Explanatory notes:

1. An e-mail address is used as display name [box (1)] as well but different from the other e-mail address [box (2)];

2. The return e-mail address in box (2) does not point to the same provider as that of box (1);

3. The first is a free public e-mail from yahoo in Hong Kong and the latter is from a media communication services provider in the US;

From: shellremittance_dept2008@yahoo.com.hk (1) [mailto:annholtz@mchsi.com] (2)
Sent: Friday, 22 August 2008 10:33 PM
To: info@shell.com (3)
Subject: Award Final Notification!!! (4)

YOU HAVE WON THE SHELL LOTTERY INTERNATIONAL ONLINE PROMO, you have therefore be approved (5) for a lump sum pay out of $2,000,000.00 (Two Million USD),contact our claims agent;Mr.Johnson Cole.
E-Mail:shellremittance_dept2008@yahoo.com.hk (6)

4. Apparently used a genuine-like address [box (3)] at the 'To:' field perhaps to fake authenticity. There were possibly multiple recipients in the 'Bcc:' field;

5. Other usual patterns include a notification [box (4)], a story with errors [box (5)] and a contact e-mail [box (6)]. Incidentally, the e-mails [boxes (1) & (6)] seem to match for a change. However that does not necessarily make this e-mail a genuine notification.

Example 2 – Nokia Email Promotion

Explanatory notes:

1. This is an example of yet another trick that scammers adopt to obfuscate the tracking of the source of their e-mail [box (1)]. Information similar to what appears in a normal e-mail header is planted to confuse detection of the source or path it has taken;

< 62 >

2. Other identifiable patterns in this e-mail include a story, asking you to contact an agent [box (4)] with details [box (5)] and a contact e-mail address [box (6)] that is from one of the many free (public) web based services. A standard warning [box (7)] tries to make the e-mail look like legitimate too perhaps;

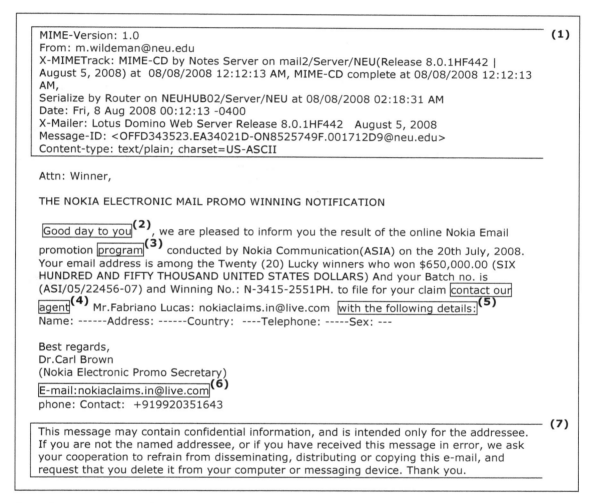

MIME-Version: 1.0   **(1)**
From: m.wildeman@neu.edu
X-MIMETrack: MIME-CD by Notes Server on mail2/Server/NEU(Release 8.0.1HF442 |
August 5, 2008) at 08/08/2008 12:12:13 AM, MIME-CD complete at 08/08/2008 12:12:13
AM,
Serialize by Router on NEUHUB02/Server/NEU at 08/08/2008 02:18:31 AM
Date: Fri, 8 Aug 2008 00:12:13 -0400
X-Mailer: Lotus Domino Web Server Release 8.0.1HF442   August 5, 2008
Message-ID: <OFFD343523.EA34021D-ON8525749F.001712D9@neu.edu>
Content-type: text/plain; charset=US-ASCII

Attn: Winner,

THE NOKIA ELECTRONIC MAIL PROMO WINNING NOTIFICATION

Good day to you **(2)**, we are pleased to inform you the result of the online Nokia Email
promotion program **(3)** conducted by Nokia Communication(ASIA) on the 20th July, 2008.
Your email address is among the Twenty (20) Lucky winners who won $650,000.00 (SIX
HUNDRED AND FIFTY THOUSAND UNITED STATES DOLLARS) And your Batch no. is
(ASI/05/22456-07) and Winning No.: N-3415-2551PH. to file for your claim contact our
agent **(4)** Mr.Fabriano Lucas: nokiaclaims.in@live.com with the following details: **(5)**
Name: ------Address: ------Country: ----Telephone: -----Sex: ---

Best regards,
Dr.Carl Brown
(Nokia Electronic Promo Secretary)
E-mail:nokiaclaims.in@live.com **(6)**
phone: Contact: +919920351643

This message may contain confidential information, and is intended only for the addressee. **(7)**
If you are not the named addressee, or if you have received this message in error, we ask
your cooperation to refrain from disseminating, distributing or copying this e-mail, and
request that you delete it from your computer or messaging device. Thank you.

3. The greeting [box (2)] and the spelling [box (3)] if taken together may indicate that the mail has probably been sent from Australia or has some connection with Australia;

4. The domain identified in the e-mail address [box (1)], which may have been spoofed is apparently from the *Northeastern University* in Boston and may have been used to once again confuse the source;

< 63 >

5. Needless to say that there has been no e-mail promotion of any kind from Nokia.

Example 3 – International Awareness Promotion from BMW

From: BMW AUTOMOBILE COMPANY **(1)** [chbennett@eircom.net] **(2)**
Sent: Tuesday, 29 July 2008 10:21 PM
To: info@bmw.com **(3)**
Subject: CONFIRM YOUR BMW PRIZE **(4)**.

THE INTERNATIONAL AWARENESS PROMOTION
DEPARTMENT OF THE BMW AUTOMOBILE COMPANY.
22 Garden Close, Stamford, Lincs, PE9 2YP, London
United Kingdom.

(5)

The Board of Directors, members of staff and the International Awareness Promotion Department of the BMW Automobile Company, wishes to congratulate you on your success as one of our TEN(10) STAR PRIZE WINNER in this years'BMW Automobile International Awareness Promotion(IAP) held on Sunday 27TH of July, 2008,in London. This makes you a proud owner of a brand new BMW 5 Series, M Sport Saloon car and a cash prize of #750,000.00 GBP (Seven Hundred and Fifty Thousand Great British pounds).

Note: You are to keep your winnings and the following below strictly confidential **(6)** so as to avoid double claims and complications: Reference Number: BMW:2551256003/23 Ticket number: 5647600545188 Serial number: BMWP/556543450906

(7)

For you to collect your prizes, kindly fill the verification form below and send it to the BMW Claims Manager, Mr. David Brown of our claims office through email, stating your receipt of this notification. He has been mandated to offer you assistance and facilitate the urgent delivery of your prizes.

MR. DAVID BROWN

TEL: +447045703610
TEL: +447045718030
EMAIL:bmwheadofffice1@hotmail.com **(8)**

(9)

VERIFICATION FORM:

1.) FULL NAME:
2.) AGE:
3.) SEX:
4.) ADDRESS:
5.) COUNTRY:
6.) PHONE:
7.) OCCUPATION/POSITION:

(10)

Congratulations once more, and keep trusting BMW Automobile for topquality automobiles.

ENGR.LLOYD BRADFORD
DIRECTOR OF PROMOTIONS,
INTERNATIONAL AWARENESS PROMOTIONS,
BMW AUTOMOBILE.
LONDON, UNITED KINGDOM

< 64 >

Explanatory notes:

1. As mentioned in examples so far, the display name [box (1)] appears just a made-up name without any connection to the e-mail address [box (2)], which incidentally points to an Irish ISP;

2. It is more than likely that this e-mail has been sent to multiple recipients. The e-mail address against 'To:' field [box (2)] may be genuine and perhaps used only to misguide those recipients;

3. Other tell-tale patterns include an implied claim [box (4)], a story [box (5)], requesting confidentiality [box (6)], nominating an agent [box (7)], a web based free public e-mail address [box (8)] as the designated contact, and a verification form [box (9)] seeking personal information.

The e-mail finally adds a congratulatory line [box (10)] perhaps to make it look real; however the patterns discussed above should undeniably prove to any sceptic that the e-mail is an attempted SCAM.

< 65 >

Philanthropy/Charity SCAMs

Example 1 – Run this Charity

Explanatory notes:

1. The story appears a standard trick to initiate a dialog and take victim(s) for a ride eventually;

From: Daniel Thums **(1)** [mailto:leonor.pino@tie.cl] **(2)**
Sent: Monday, 11 August 2008 12:38 AM
Subject: Philanthropy Assistance **(3)**

Dear Friend,

My name is Mr.Daniel Thums,I apologize for the manner in which I contacted you.I got your email address from one of the email addresses on to several email prayers and jokes that are usually forwarded to me by well-wishers in other **(4)** to keep my spirits up.

I am 65yrs old of age.I am a resident of New York City in the United States of America.I am a business Man as I have spent all my life on corporate investment business in England.Earlier this year I was diagnosed with lung cancer, with this condition,I find it uneasy to survive myself, because my investments can not be run and managed efficiently by me as it is when I was still active.In this circumstances, I have decided to help the less privileged and those that needs help financially.If you need any financial support or have theintention of helping those needy around you,don't fail to contact me back,because I am willing to help.

If you are interested and you have the time to spare,you can assist me in running this charity **(5)** Organization and distribute the funds that I'm willing to release to interested individual that wants to set up a philanthropy project in their community.You may as well volunteer or for pay as we may agree upon. Do get in touch with me as soon as you can to enable me give you more information **(6)** of what is to be done.Respond to me through this email address(philanthropyproject2000@yahoo.com **(7)**). Your immediate responds **(8)** will be appreciated.

Remain Blessed,
Daniel Thums **(9)**

---

2. Like in other examples listed so far, the patterns in this e-mail pointing to a SCAM include an attention grabber [box (3)], a story, a few errors [boxes (4) & (8)], a direction to contact someone [box (6)] and a contact e-mail address [box (7)];

3. After seeing matching names [boxes (1) & (9)] and reading other information contained within this story, kind hearted readers may think that this e-mail is genuine. Especially so, if he/she has been working with some charities or generally inclined to help others;

< 66 >

4. However, if you look closely, you may note that the e-mail address [box (2)] figures in another e-mail SCAM listed (page 60) in example 7 under 'Lottery SCAMs';

5. After a prospective victim contacts the sender of this e-mail or his/her agent, the sequence of operation could be more or less same like other varieties of SCAMs;

6. Hence all advisories suggest not responding to such e-mails at all.

Example 2 – Dispatch to the Poor

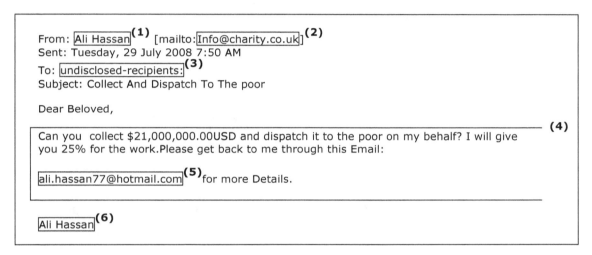

Explanatory notes:

1. By its very construction of the story [box (4)] in this e-mail, this example appears a bit more obvious and hence a straight forward SCAM to identify;

2. The patterns of multiple recipients and a contact e-mail address from a free web based service [boxes (3) & (5)] are all there;

3. On further inspection, one would also note that there is no domain registered as 'charity.co.uk' and hence it appears fake;

4. The modus operandi seems to be first asking for some *small* handling fee to release the quoted amount; and then continuing like other AFF type frauds with demands for more money under various other pretexts.

< 67 >

Example 3 – A Wish from Deathbed

From: Mrs. Rose Ibrahim [mailto:mrroseibrahim22@yahoo.de] **(1)**
Sent: Tuesday, 29 July 2008 9:50 AM
Subject: PLEASE STAND AS THE BENEFICIARY TO MY FUNDS **(2)**

Dear Beloved One.

It is by the grace of God that I see today, as I have not particularly lived my life so well, as I never really cared for anyone (not even myself) but my business. Having known the truth; I had no choice than to do what is lawful **(3)** and just in the sight of God for eternal life and in the sight of man for witness of God & His Mercies and glory upon my life.

— **(4)**

I am Mrs. Rose Ibrahim, the wife of Late Mr. El Ibrahim, My husband worked with the Chevron/Texaco in Russia for twenty years before he died in the year 2004.We were married for ten years without a child.

My Husband died after a brief illness that lasted for only four days. Since his death I decided not to re-marry or get a child outside my matrimonial home, When my late husband was alive he deposited the sum of 7.5 Million Pounds (Seven Million Five Hundred Thousand Pounds) with a Bank in Europe.

Presently, this money is still with the Bank and the management just wrote me as the beneficiary that our account has been DORMANT and if I, as the beneficiary of the funds, do not re-activate the account; the funds will be CONFISCATED or I rather issue a letter of authorization to somebody to receive it on my behalf (note that you need to activate this account) as I can not come over. Presently, I'm in a hospital in Russia where I have been undergoing treatment for esophageal cancer. I have since lost my ability to talk and my doctors have told me that I have only a few weeks to live.

It is my last wish to see this money distributed to charity organizations **(5)** anywhere in the World in helping human race.

Because relatives and friends have plundered so much of my wealth since my illness, I cannot live with the agony of entrusting this huge responsibility to any of them. Please, I beg you in the name of God to help me Stand-in as the beneficiary and collect the Funds from the Bank **(6)**.

I took this decision because I don't have any child that will inherit this money, and I am not afraid of death since I know where I am going to. I don't need any telephone communication in this regard because of mysoundless voice and presence of my husband's relatives around me always **(7)**. I don't want them to know about this development.

I await your quick response **(8)** to this mail as this is my last wish **(9)** to see this funds transferred before my Death. Please my beloved for further communication on how we are going to conclude this **(10)**, reach me on my private mail:

mrroseibrahim_22@yahoo.de **(11)**

Remain Blessed

Your Beloved Sister .
Mrs. Rose Ibrahim **(12)**

< 68 >

Explanatory notes:

1. There are many good-hearted people out there who might believe this story mainly because of the way it was presented;

2. Initial misgivings [box (2) & (4)] may give way to sympathy, particularly because of what is stated in [boxes (3), (5), (6) & (9)] here;

3. The name is matching [boxes (1) & (12)] as well;

4. But let us have a second read. What is written in here [boxes (7), (8), (10) & (11)] is sufficient to confirm that this is nothing but an AFF type SCAM;

5. Anyone who is falling for these types of stories (and the huge amount of money that would be mentioned therein) whether out of sympathy or otherwise, will definitely part with his/her hard-earned money at the end for sure;

6. Please read the notes for the previous example, particularly the last one.

< 69 >

Seeking Help to Commit Fraud

Example 1 – Mutual Benefit

From: Mr.Duka Dawodu **(1)** [mailto:andovale@paraisonet.com.br] **(2)**
Sent: Monday, 18 August 2008 12:44 AM
Cc: recipient list not shown: **(3)**
Subject: Mutual Benefit **(4)**

Hello,

— **(5)**

My name is Duka Dawodu, and I hope my business proposal **(6)** will be a pleasant surprise to you, as we have had no prior business relationship before now.First let me place upfront by letting you know that this proposal is not a scam **(7)** and will not in future time be related to any term mark illegal **(8)** and it is 100% risk free.I am from United Kingdom, I am sixty-five years old and a Vice President in a major bank here in the United Kingdom where I stumbled on this remarkable discovery I am about to share with you.On November 6, 2004, a Canadian Oil consultant/contractor with the Liberian National Petroleum Corporation (LNPC), MR.BARRY KELLY made a Fixed Deposit for twelve calendar months, valued at US$125,000,000.00 (ONE HUNDRED AND TWENTY FIVE MILLION UNITED STATE DOLLARS) in my bank.

Upon maturity, I sent a routine notification to his forwarding address but got no reply. Several periodic reminders were sent but to no avail and finally we discovered from his contract employers, the Liberian National Petroleum Corpration **(9)** that MR.BARRY KELLY died from an automobile accident.

Further investigation revealed that Late BARRY KELLY declared no next of kin on his sworn affidavits with the bank records. This sum of US$125,000,000.00 is still in my bank here in the United Kingdom accumulating interest yet unclaimed till date. According to Laws and Constitution, the government could confiscate this money if unclaimed for another two years. I am therefore, most humbly and discreetly seeking a reliable, honest and trustworthy foreign associate and friend to help take delivery and secure these funds on my behalf **(10)**, with the intention of investing in a possible profitable business in your country under your directive and supervision of SIR.DAVE JOHNSON. Rather than having it seized by the authorities.

The details of these and the manner these resources shall be transferred from my bank to your bank account which you shall provide **(11)** would be discussed during your meeting **(12)** with SIR.DAVE JOHNSON all follow-up and dialogue prior to this projectwill be forward **(13)** to you upon receipt of your reply **(14)** to SIR.DAVE JOHNSON (sir.davej@yahoo.com **(15)**) he shall be making available to you more details **(16)** that will help you understand the transaction better. Please realize that I cannot divulge too much at this stage because of the office i am occupying **(17)**.

Thanks for your time and I hope to be hearing from you soon.

Regards,
Mr.Duka Dawodu **(18)**

< 70 >

Explanatory notes:

1. This is a very easily identifiable SCAM. The story [box (5)] is suspicious because of its presentation itself from the very start;

2. While it portrays the inquiry as a business proposal of mutual interest, legal and risk-free [boxes (4), (6), (7) & (8)], it contradicts itself by asking you to participate in outright fraud in a non-ambiguous manner [boxes (10), (11) & (17)];

3. Further, you have been invited to contact another [boxes (12), (14), (15) & (16)]. Please review comments earlier (page 59) about the potential risks of meeting [box (12)] any of the scammers;

4. The e-mail address [box (2)] can be traced to an ISP in Brazil and may have been spoofed or by unauthorised access;

5. The fact that the mail has been sent to many recipients [box (3] demonstrates that this is nothing but an e-mail SCAM;

6. Finally, this whole story and the name of the sender [boxes (1) & 18)] have been flagged by many bloggers and news-groups as a definite SCAM.

Example 2 – Help This Charity

Explanatory notes:

1. Despite the subtlety of the presentation in this example, readers will be able to spot those usual patterns of deception throughout the text of this e-mail;

2. The story [box (2)] is same as that of above with very minor modifications except that the recipient is requested to contact the same person as the sender [boxes (1) & (13)];

3. The scammer seems to be underestimating the intelligence of others by suggesting that anyone can be nominated as the inheritor of a total stranger and that it would still be legal and legitimate [boxes (4) & (6)];

< 71 >

From: Jeremiah Gwan [mailto:drgwan@msn.com] **(1)**
Sent: Wednesday, 13 August 2008 1:24 PM
Subject: Indicate your interest
Importance: High

Dear Friend

Thank you for reading this email.

——————————————————————————————————————— **(2)**

With apologies for interference in your email privacy I am Dr. Jeremiah Gwan, a charity health worker and Director HolyChild Foundation here in Ghana. I am writing you with regard to a Late good friend of mine and founder of the Foundation, who was a foreigner from your part of the world and the managing director of an investment firm here in Ghana Unfortunately he died in 2000, He established these foundation to help less privileged minority people in our society which it was doing pretty well before the unfortunate death of its founder.

I am to conduct a standard process Investigation/Recommendation on behalf of the Investment Banking Department of The Trust Bank Ghana. This involves our founder and the circumstances surrounding redeemable 10 year Bonds in form of Government Treasury Bills which he bought with its Funds Redemption date since due for Payment, the bank contacted me a month ago as the director of his foundation and a trustee to recommend a next of kin to the funds valued at US$3,000,000 (Three Million Dollars) since he (Our Late founder) died intestate and nominated no successor in title over the fund.

The essence of this communication with you is to request that you provide me with information/comments **(3)** on any or all of the two issues as regards nominating you to inherit the fund left behind since you are also a foreigner with the same surname hence eligible to stand for claim of the funds. I have therefore contacted you to be legally nominated **(4)** as next of kin (inheritor) to Our Late founder after all inquiries and investigation even with the relevant embassy has yielded results showing that there is no known or living next of kin. You are required therefore to answer this questions **(5)** to enable me make my recommendation to The Trust Bank Ghana.

Can you confirm your willingness to accept this inheritance if you are legally and legitimately nominated **(6)** through my recommendation to the bank and approved to stand as inheritor to this funds. Would you agree to donate 60% of this inheritance **(7)** to our charity organization if you are officially recommended to the bank in my powers to stand as the Inheritor?.

It is pertinent that you inform me ASAP **(8)** whether or not you are familiar with this personality or and your interest **(9)** towards the issues mentioned. You must appreciate that I am constrained from providing you with more detailed information at this point **(10)**.

Please respond to this mail as soon as possible **(11)** to afford me the opportunity to provide you with more information **(12)** on matter and upon your consent proceed with the recommendation of your person to the bank as the inheritor of the fund.

Thank you for accommodating this inquiry.

Remain Blessed.

Dr. Jeremiah Gwan **(13)**
+233246917036
HolyChild Foundation **(14)**.

< 72 >

4. The plot becomes clearer [boxes (3), (5), (8), (9), (10), (11) & (12)] as you read that the recipient can keep 40% of the amount as a reward (?) for his/her part [box (7)] in the fraud;

5. There are remarkable similarities [boxes (10) & (12)] from the earlier example (page 70) too;

6. Incidentally, the charity mentioned in this e-mail seems to be an adaptation of Holy Child Foundation, a Catholic educational trust operating in many western countries. At the end of the day, this e-mail above seems yet another attempted SCAM and nothing else.

Example 3 – Request from Russia

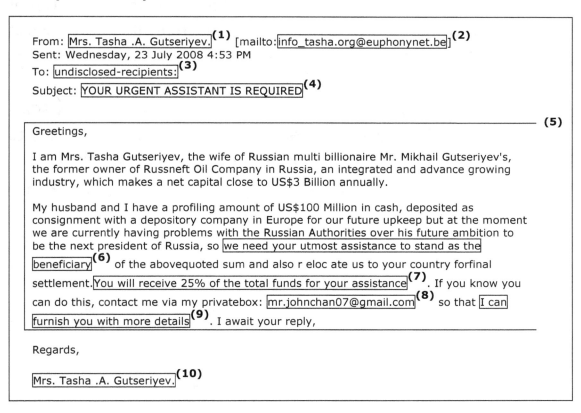

Explanatory notes:

1. This appears yet another straight forward case of an e-mail SCAM with all usual ingredients [boxes (3) to (10)] as in other examples listed in this book;

< 73 >

2. Incidentally, the e-mail address [box (2)] points to an ISP in Belgium and the other e-mail address [box (8)] perhaps adds a Chinese (?) connection.

Example 4 – Perfectly Legal

Explanatory notes:

1. A bit more serious e-mail SCAM with potential adverse consequences whether one responds or not, mainly because it was addressed to the recipient [box (2)] directly;

2. Hence the recipient's e-mail address [box (2)] has been removed;

3. Whether or not the scammer really has the details [box (4) & (7)] of the recipient may only be a matter of conjecture. It is nevertheless worrying because of the Australian [box (4)] flavour and the fact that the recipient lives in Australia too;

4. The long story [box (5)] however has all the ingredients of a SCAM throughout and all typical patterns [boxes (3), (8), (9) and (11) to (20)] including errors [boxes (6) & (10)] as found in other cases;

5. Readers may have noted that the private e-mail address [box (19)] is from a Microsoft portal.

< 74 >

From: Barrister Smith Anderson [mailto:smith_andersonchambers@smith.com] **(1)**
Sent: Wednesday, 23 July 2008 6:51 PM
To: <<<removed>>> **(2)**
Subject: FOR YOUR KIND AND URGENT ATTENTION. **(3)**

Good Day, **(4)**

_____ **(5)**

I am sorry for bothering you and please do not be surprised at this mail but I crave your indulgence to just give it fair attention to convince yourself. I am Barr. Smith Anderson, a solicitor at law. I am the personal attorney to Scott Kennedy, a foreigner who was an oil merchant here and used to work with Handebull Construction & Oil Services in Nigeria hereinafter referred to as my client.

On the 6th of May, 2002 it was reported to us that my Client and his wife were involved in a Local Plane Crash at Kano State en route from Sokoto to Abuja (the capital city of Nigeria), all occupants in the Plane lost their lives, unfortunately on this same flight were other dignitaries like the former Nigeria Sports Minister and a host of others . Since then I have made several inquiries to the embassies here to locate any of my clients extended relations, these effort **(6)** proved unsuccessful. After these several unsuccessful attempts, I decided to contact you after looking at your profile **(7)** and believing we can work together to actualize this dream **(8)** , hence I contacted you and I feel it is by divine providence that I am contacting you in this matter. I have contacted you to assist in repatriating the fund **(9)** valued at US$10.5 million left behind by my client before it gets confiscated or declared unserviceable by the bank , where my late client operated his account. The bank has since issued me a notice, to provide the next of kin or have the account confiscated by their next board meeting. For the fact that I have been unsuccessful in locating the relatives during these past period **(10)** of time, I seek your consent to present you as the next of kin to the deceased **(11)** and now that I have finally located you, I honestly think it does not matter even if you are not related to my late client **(12)** the MOST IMPORTANT thing is that you are INTERESTED to execute the matter with me and since he did not leave any record behind even at the bank, i will have no problem to convince the bank that you are related to him because it is better for you and me to claim this money than for the bank to seize it as unclaimed **(13)** .

I will present you to the bank as a COUSIN to my late client and I will secure all necessary legal documents to back up this claim so that the proceeds of this account can be paid to you, instead of the bank confiscating the money. I feel the money will be more useful to you and me than the bank. Therefore, on receipt of your positive response **(14)** , we shall then discuss the modalities for transfer and I will give you the full details **(15)** . I have all necessary information and have arranged to process all the relevant legal documents needed to back you up **(16)** for the claim. All I require from you, is your honest co-operation to enable us see this transaction through. I guarantee that this will be executed under a legitimate arrangement, that will protect you from any breach of the law and as we progress, you will also have the opportunity to confirm directly from the bank **(17)** about this deposit.

_____

IMPORTANT: For more privacy of your reply. PLEASE REPLY **(18)** TO MY PERSONAL EMAIL: smith_anderson2591@live.com **(19)**

(THIS EMAIL IS MORE PRIVATE TO ME) and I will give you my telephone number **(20)** for more details.

Respectfully,
Barrister Smith Anderson. **(21)**

< 75 >

Other 'Nigerian' SCAMs

Example 1 – UN Compensates SCAM Victims

From: ANTI-FRAUD TEAM**(1)** [mailto:mikeokri06@gmail.com]**(2)**
Sent: Tuesday, 26 August 2008 2:28 AM
Subject: GOOD NEWS!**(3)**

Attention:
_____ **(4)**

How are you today? Hope all is well with you and your family?,You may not understand why this mail came to you.

We have been having meetings for the passed**(5)** 7 months which ended 14 days ago with the former secretary**(6)** to the United Nations (UN).

This email is to all the people that have been scammed/defrauded in any part of the world, the United Nations have agreed to compensate them with the sum of US$ 100,000**(7)**. This includes every foreign contractor that may have not received their contract sum, and people that had an unfinished transactions**(8)** or international business that failed due to Government problems etc.

We found your name in our list**(9)** that is why we are contacting you,this has been agreed upon and has been signed.

You are advised to contact Mr. Jim Ovia of ZENITH BANK NIGERIA PLC,**(10)** as he is our representative in Nigeria. Contact him immediately**(11)** for your Cheque/ International Bank Draft of US$ 100,000.

These funds are in a Bank Draft for security purpose.He will send it to you,after which you clear it in any bank of your choice**(12)**.

Therefore, you should send him your full Name and telephone number/your correct mailing address where you want him to send the Draft to you**(13)**.

Contact Mr. Jim Ovia immediately for your Cheque:

Email: jim1ovia@gmail.com**(14)**

Phone: +234 802 450 7773

Thank you and God bless you and your family. Hoping to hear from you as soon as you have your Bank Draft cashed**(15)**.

Making the world a better place

Regards,
Mike Okri
ANTI-FRAUD TEAM**(16)**

< 76 >

Explanatory notes:

1. This perhaps is an over-ambitious – if not cruel – SCAM to defraud a previous victim further. Unfortunately many victims still seem to fall for such a claim that the UN has decided to compensate victims globally;

2. The modus operandi of scammer(s) could be slightly different here from what is a typical AFF type SCAM as listed before;

3. Invariably the scammer(s) will send their victim(s) a cheque, often with a figure more than the quoted amount in the e-mail. Then as if the accountant made a mistake, victim(s) will be asked to wire back the amount in error immediately;

4. An unsuspecting victim would normally oblige because he/she has already got a cheque and may not doubt the communication;

5. Only when the cheque bounces – which normally takes a couple of weeks – victim(s) realise that the international cheque that he/she received was fake, leaving the victim(s) to pay a dishonour fee to his/her bank in addition to what he/she already sent the scammer(s) towards refunding an apparent overpayment;

6. Otherwise, this e-mail also has all usual patterns that one can spot in other e-mail SCAMs. They include a story [boxes (4), (10), (11), (12) & (15)], errors [boxes (5), (6) & (8)], seeking your contact details [box (13)] and a contact e-mail address [box (14)] of the public (free to join) variety;

7. Readers may have noted that the display name [box (1)] is a made-up string without any apparent connection to the e-mail address [box (2)] that was used to send this e-mail. The *gmail* is a public (free to join) e-mail service from Google. Nor does it [box (2)] have any correlation to such a claim that the mail is from anti-fraud team [box (16)] and/or from UN.

< 77 >

Example 2 – You Have a Package

From: Mrs. Virgil Storrs **(1)** [mailto:info@online-fedex.com]**(2)**
Sent: Tuesday, 29 July 2008 9:54 PM
To: unlisted-recipients:**(3)** ; no To-header on input**(4)**
Subject: You Have A Package: Contact FedEx!**(5)**

Greetings!

(6)

I have been waiting for you since to contact me for your Confirmable Bank Draft of $800.000.00**(7)** United States Dollars,but I did not hear from you since that time. Then I went and deposited the Draft with FedEx COURIER SERVICE,West Africa**(8)** ,I travelled out of the country for a 3 Months Course and I will not come back till end of August**(9)**. What you have to do now is to contact the FedEx COURIER SERVICE as soon as possible**(10)** to know when they will deliver your package to you because of the expiring date**(11)**. For your information, I have paid for the delivering Charge**(12)**, Insurance premium and Clearance Certificate Fee of the Cheque showing that it is not a Drug Money or meant to sponsor Terrorist attack in your Country.

The only money you will send to the FedEx COURIER SERVICE to deliver your Draft direct to your postal Address in your country is ($180.00 USD)**(13)** only being Security Keeping Fee of the Courier Company**(14)** so far. Again, don't be deceived by anybody to pay any other money except $180.00 USD Dollars**(15)**. I would have paid that but they said no because they don't know when you willcontact them and in case of demurrage**(16)**. You have to contact the FedEx COURIER SERVICE now for the delivery of your Draft with this information bellow;

Contact Person: Mr. Benny Blunt**(17)**
Email Address:fedex_delivery68@yahoo.com.hk**(18)**
Telephone: +2348057547555.

Finally, make sure that you reconfirm your Postal address; Direct telephone number; Do send it to them again**(19)** to avoid any mistake on the Delivery and ask them to give you the tracking number to enable you track your package over there and know when it will get to your address. Let me repeat again**(20)**, try to contact them as soon as you receive this mail to avoid any further delay**(21)** and remember to pay them their Security Keeping fee of $180.00 US Dollars for their immediate action**(22)**. You should also let me know through email as soon as you receive your Draft**(23)**.

Yours Faithfully,
Mrs. Virgil Storrs**(24)**

Explanatory notes:

1. Readers may recollect that the display name is same as in an earlier example under 'A Benevolent Aunt' (page 49). There are only very few differences between these two e-mails in the text too;

< 78 >

2. The 'Security Keeping Fee' has been increased from USD 100.00 in the earlier example to USD 180.00 [boxes (13), (15) & (22)] in this e-mail above;

3. Name of the contact person has been changed, contact details have changed and Mrs. Storrs has an e-mail address with an 'online-fedex' in it. This is perhaps to mislead recipient(s) of this e-mail towards taking it for a genuine communication;

4. The amount earlier was one million USD and in this e-mail the amount is only USD 800,000;

5. Other than that the story [box (6)] seems to be kept the same even word for word [boxes (3), (8) to (10), (15), (16), (19), etc] including the error [box (11)]. The *delivering Charge* [box (12)] seems to be a new addition;

6. Readers may want to compare the rest of the marked patterns with earlier examples.

Example 3 – Sonangol Oil Exploration

Explanatory Notes:

1. The display name and the e-mail address do not match [boxes (1) & (2)];

2. The e-mail address [box (2)] points to an ISP – or the only ISP – in Bangladesh. The address could have been spoofed or the scammer(s) may have broken into their system;

3. This mail is possibly sent to multiple recipients [box (3)];

4. Unemployed people may fall for this factor of urgency [box (4)] and make decisions without a detailed examination of the rest;

5. Spelling and grammatical errors [boxes (5), (6), (7), (8), (10) & (11)] in the construction of the scammer's story used to be a very telling pattern; however, recent e-mails seem to be well constructed. See other examples in this book;

< 79 >

6. The recipients are asked to contact a public e-mail address [box (9)], which the scammer(s) may have registered under fake identity. It does not seem to have any connection with the employer described in the story any way;

From: THE HUMAN RESOURCES DEPT SONANGOL OIL PLC **(1)**
[mailto:tby@bangla.net] **(2)**
Sent: Thursday, 24 July 2008 12:03 AM
To: undisclosed-recipients: **(3)**
Subject: SONANGOL OIL EMPLOYMENT OFFER APPLICANT NEEDED URGENTLY **(4)**

SONANGOL OIL CORPORATION.

The global oil gas and petrochemical giant has stated drilling for oil in Angola's $3.5 billion kizomba C and D project, 322 kilometers offshore.The project, the largest offshore Africa, came onstream about few months ahead of schedule.

SONANGOL OIL CORPORATION has vacancy for reputable an **(5)** qualified individuals, as we are about to embark on a project which will require expatriates in the following profession. engineering,instrumentation, information technology and enviromental/safety sciences. The engineering aspect of the project still requires personnels **(6)** who are trained and experinced **(7)** in the following areas:Petroleum engineering, structural engineering,electrical/electronics engineering, machanical engineering, civil engineering, instrumentation engineering, enviromental engineering, Welders,technicians, electricians, plumbers, pipefilters, drivers, nurses, computer engineers and computer programmers etc.to complete the required number of expatriates.Services of expatriates who are trained and skilled in project management and contract administrator are also required including those in the administrative and management status.

Do send the following requirment **(8)** to Vincent Griffey (Through the president email address on sonangoloilplc1@yahoo.co.uk **(9)** telling him your
(1)Name
(2)Country
(3 Cell phone number
(4 Sex:
(5)Home phone number:
(6 Present job.
(7 Resume/curriculum vitae.

We hereby look foward **(10)** to the reciept **(11)** of expatriates to make up the team.

Regards,
Mcvelly Richard
FOR SONANGOL OIL CORPORATION.

---
(12)

Sonangol is managed by the:Administration Council - has the overall responsibility for the management of the company and is the primary decision-making body in matters of overall strategy and the authorization for investment expenditures for Sonangol Group. The Administration Council answers to Sonangol's shareholder - the government.
Financial Council - oversees and manages Sonangol Group's fiscal responsibility.
Advisory Council - provides counselling and recommendations for Sonangol Group's management.

< 80 >

7. The gobbledygook [box (12)] about the employer is perhaps to make it look like a genuine correspondence.

Normally, an employer may refer any prospective applicant to their web site for their advertisement but it is quite unlikely for it to waste time sending a SPAM-like message as above.

Example 4 – Forest Park Hotels

As a rule, any e-mail typed in all capitals could be SPAM. In *cyber* world a message in all capitals is said to be analogous to *shouting* as a means of communication in the real world. The next example is one in which the message is in all capitals with other tell-tale patterns, making it a suspected SCAM mail.

Explanatory Notes:

1. The display name and the e-mail address from where this e-mail probably came [(boxes (1) & (2)] have no apparent correlation as usual in e-mail SCAMs;

2. The e-mail has the same address in both 'From:' and 'To:' fields [boxes (2) & (3)], which points to a news portal in Brazil;

3. The contents appear to be a blanket *cover-all* type of job advertisement;

4. The most frightening aspect of this is that it asks a prospective applicant to send a scanned copy of his/her international passport [box (4)] even before viewing any resume or CV;

5. The e-mail address of the 'Admin Manager' [box (5)] points to a portal in Poland;

6. Whatever the sender wanted to say here [box (6)], it does not make much sense;

7. Notwithstanding the snail-mail address, the whole message does not appear genuine.

< 81 >

SPAM 2 SCAM

From: INTER TAT **(1)** [mailto:uuuu1112@ig.com.br] **(2)**
Sent: Thursday, 24 July 2008 2:20 AM
To: uuuu1112@ig.com.br **(3)**
Subject: EMPLOYMENT OPPORTUNITY

FOREST PARK HOTELS
33,MARKET STREET, ATHERTON, MANCHESTER M46 0RE,
UNITED KINGDOM.

WE ARE LOOKING FOR BRIGHT GRADUATES/POST GRADUATES BETWEEN AGES 22 AND
ABOVE YEARS WITH EXCELLENT COMMUNICATION AND MANAGERIAL SKILLS AND AN
APTITUDE FOR CUSTOMER SERVICES. CANDIDATES WOULD BE REQUIRED TO POSSES
GOOD INTER-PERSONAL SKILLS AND A PASSION TO KEEP LEARNING WHILE DELIVERING
EFFECTIVE SERVICES TO OUR NUMEROUS CUSTOMERS,YOU WILL BE WORKING
PRIMARILY IN ROTATING DAY SHIFTS,WITH OCCASIONAL NIGHT SHIFTS. VACANCIES
ARE AVAILABLE IN THE FOLLOWING DEPUTATIONS:

1. MANAGERS/ASSISTANT MANAGERS
2. COMPUTER OPERATORS/SOFTWARE ENGINEERS
3. ACCOUNTANTS
4. SECURITY
5. LINGUISTS
6. CASHIERS
7. ESCORTS
8. CHEFS
9. SUPERVISOR TRAINERS
10. WAITERS
11. CLEANERS

ENTITLEMENTS, BENEFITS & PACKAGES: A VERY ATTRACTIVE NET SALARY PAID IN GBP
[GREAT BRITAIN POUNDS]. QUALITY SINGLE OR FAMILY HOUSING ACCOMODATIONS IN
HOTEL VICINITY. FREE MEDICAL CARE FOR EMPLOYEE AND FAMILY HERE IN LONDON .
EXCELLENT EDUCATIONAL ASSISTANCE BENEFITS WITH FAMILY STATUS EMPLOYMENT.

PAID AIRFARES ALLOWING FULL FLEXIBILITY WITH HOLIDAYS. PERSONAL EFFECTS
SHIPMENTS AND EXCESS BAGGAGE ALLOWANCES FULL ACCESS TO SOME OF THE BEST
RECREATIONAL FACILITIES IN LONDON LIFE INSURANCES. OFFICIAL VEHICLES /MAXIMUM
SECURITY IN WORK ENVIRONS AND HOUSING COMMUNITY.

JOB STATUS: FULL TIME AND CONTRACT [PLEASE INDICATE WHEN APPLYING].

SALARY INDICATION:GBP 2,500 TO GBP 4,500 MONTHLY DEPENDING ON
EXPERIENCE,FIELD OF SPECIALIZATION.INTERESTED CANDIDATES SHOULD PLEASE SEND
THEIR RESUMES BY EMAIL AND ADDRESSED TO,

THE ADMIN MANAGER,
FOREST PARK HOTELS,
33,MARKET STREET, ATHERTON, MANCHESTER M46 0RE,
UNITED KINGDOM.

PLEASE ATTACH A SCANNED COPY OF YOUR INTERNATIONAL PASSPORT **(4)** TO IT WHEN
SENDING BACK THE APPLICATION FORM TO THE HOTEL ADMIN MANAGER (email;
jeanclaude2@o2.pl) **(5)**

(6)

PLEASE NOTE THE ATTACHMENT WILL BE SENT TO BE FILLED AND RETURN BY
ATTACHMENT AFTER YOUR REPLY HAS BEEN NOTIFIED.

REGARDS
ADMIN MANAGER,
MR JEAN CLAUDE. FOREST PARK HOTELS

< 82 >

Example 5 – Another Oil & Gas Project

Explanatory Notes:

1. Please see explanatory notes for previous examples for comparison;

2. Contrast the sender's details [box (1)] with the e-mail address at the end [box (14)];

3. Both are free e-mail addresses anybody could sign-up for. One of them is from Microsoft [box (1)] and the other [box (14)] is from yahoo;

4. The logo of the organisation may make it look real, but the second link has nothing to do with the first other than an 'html' file by the name of the organisation;

5. The American spelling [box (3)] may be one of the errors [see boxes (5), (6), (9), (10), & (12)] as another word [box (4)] is spelt with British spelling;

6. The salary offered [box (7)] seems to be extremely generous particularly in light of an offer to pay three month's salary upfront [box (11)] on confirmation of documents and hence it is an allurement in all probabilities to recruit unsuspecting victims (see page 12);

7. Asking only for a resume and not a copy of the passport as in the example above (page 82), but it could just be to start a dialog or hook a prospective victim;

The e-mail appears on the next page.

< 83 >

From: TECHNIPOFFSHORE . [mailto:technip_offshore_nltt@live.com] **(1)**
Sent: Friday, 25 July 2008 6:38 PM
Subject: JOB OFFER FROM TECHNIP OFFSHORE NIGERIA LIMITED?

(2)

<http://www.technip.com/english/h_img/logo_home.gif>
Technip Offshore Nigeria Ltd.
<http://goliath.ecnext.com/coms2/merc-compint-0001323072-Technip-Offshore-Nigeria-Ltd.html>

International subsidiary
4th Fl. IMB Plz., 1 Akin Adesola Str .,
Victoria Island, Lagos, Nigeria.

INTRODUCTION:

Ref: TR/EMP/EXP/VOL.IV/07
We are Legal Labor **(3)** Consultant/Recruiters to Technip Group, a foremost Oil and Gas Company. In pursuant to the service contract with our client (Technip Group) wish to invite experienced, skilled and qualified expatriates/persons for the Ogba Phase Two Project Development going on in the Federal Republic Of Nigeria, project schedule to commence work in July, 2007.

The programme **(4)** is the Developement of Ogba Phase two project, the project involves the contruction **(5)** of Four platforms and a Gas Export Pipeline that will aid optimum exploitation of the crude oil potential of the Ogba Field, as well as that of Natural Gas that is currently being flared.

TECHNIP GROUP with respect to the said project requires expatriates whose services will include the project management, engineering,procurement, construction, transportation and installation, safety, hook up and commissioning of the production platform and pipelying **(6)**.

SCOPE OF THE PROJECT: The developments of the Ogba Phase Two project.

SALARY: $10,000- $30,000.00, Monthly **(7)**, can be transferred to any Bank or Country of your choice and all transfers must be made in conformity with the existing tax situation in Nigeria.

CONTRACT DURATION: 48 months (Liable **(8)** for upward review depending on your commitment and expertise)

DURATION OF WORK PERIODS: Three months work, one month pay **(9)** leave

You will be entitle **(10)** to Three(3) months upfront salaries and relocation expenses **(11)** on confirmation of your relevant documentation for commencement of work. We would like to have your detailed resume, if this Offer is acceptable to you together with an application via email attachement **(12)** and you are to forward it to the below Email address **(13)**. We await your response in this regard.

YOUR SINCERELY,

ENGR. JUMBO FRANK IDOWU
EXPATRIATE HUMAN RESOURCES ASST. MANAGER
Technip Offshore Nigeria Ltd.International Subsidiary 4th Fl. IMB Plz., 1 Akin Adesola Str.,
Victoria Island, Lagos, Nigeria.
Phone: +234-8039373941; Office: +234-84880463
E-Mail: technipoffsore.nlt01@yahoo.com **(14)**

< 84 >

Unsavoury Employment Offers

The difference of this type of SCAMs is perhaps that victim(s) may not lose any money upfront and hence could fail to recognise the motives of scammer(s) until it is too late. Example 2 below is a typical case.

Example 1 – A One-liner

This e-mail could be a genuine invitation that was mistaken for a SCAM. However, the usage of 'we/us' and other patterns are of concern. It may or may not be *intended* as an e-mail SCAM.

```
From: <<<removed>>>
Sent: Monday, 1 September 2008 10:23 AM
To: <<<removed>>>
Subject: Urgent mail,pls(1) confirm reciept(2)

We have a job proposal for you from china,pls(3) could you get back to us(4) as soon as
possible for further details of this transaction(5).

Sincerely,

<<<removed>>>
```

The red flags have been marked but the addresses have been removed. The spelling and construction [boxes (1), (2) & (3)] errors, relatively less in number though, may indicate that this is yet another *scoping* e-mail with intentions of fraud later in the process. Asking the recipient to get back [box (4)] for further details [box (5)] may be to initiate a dialog first. Readers may want to check and compare explanatory notes with other examples in this book.

Example 2 – Looking For an Accomplice

There were media reports a few years ago that an American was arrested for some financial crime. Only then she realised that she was a victim. It seems that she was offered a part-time job to collect money on a company's behalf, deposit it in her account and sent it to the company representative abroad every quarter or similar. The scammers were apparently using her to obfuscate their money trail.

< 85 >

Palmhive Technical Textiles Limited, NTG House, Willow Road, Lenton, Nottingham. NG7 2TA. ENGLAND Tel:+447024076987; inforfabrictextile09@yahoo.co.uk **(1)**

(2)

Palmhive Technical Textiles Limited Introduce **(3)** a position of the manager (Representative) for the payment from the customers and other financial means **(4)**. We need a book-keeper in the USA , so we want to know if you will like to work online from home **(5)** and get paid weekly without leaving or it affecting your present job **(6)**. The company deals in the sale of Chippendale, Hepplewhite, Lutyens and Rennie Mackintosh, and are **(7)** ideally suited to most forms of upholstered furniture, antique, classical and contemporary design exhibition. Palmhive Technical Textiles Limited has established an enviable reputation for manufacturing tradition of horsehair weaving and we have clients we supply weekly in the USA. We have been receiving orders from United States. Which we have not been able to process competently and completely since we do not have a payment receiving personnel in States **(8)**. We have decided to recruit payment officers online hence we will be needing a Representative/Bookkeeper to process our payments in the USA. - due to delays in processing payments from the USA in London Uk.

WHAT WE OFFER: Two hours/day at your choice, daytime or evening time **(9)**.
WORK AT HOME: Checking e-mail and going to the bank Part time or full time **(10)**.
OTHER HIGHLIGHTS: No selling involved, no kit to buy,we won't charge you anything **(11)**.

(12)

MONTHLY SALARY: Minimum of $400 every week to a total of $1600 per month AND also the total amount you make in a month depends on how often you receive payments from out Clients,which can be twice a week or more,and also pay you $2 per day for checking your email.

COMMISSION: 10% of every money order/check that is cashed instantly"cash inhand"or "cash on counter" is what you get from the total cashed amount **(13)**.

MORE EXPLANATION ABOUT THE JOB: If you receive a check of $2,500.00 from our clients or costumers **(14)** in the USA ,you would cash the check in your bank **(15)** and then take 10% which is $250,from it and then send the rest of the funds from it to anywhere in the world where the company delegates would be at that time **(16)**.

OTHER FEES: All the cost for the transfer of the money to any location in the world where the Palmhive Technical Textiles Limited delegate would be,shall also be deducted from the total funds left with you after you have deducted your Commission which is 10% of any amount you cash and then you send the remainder of the funds as you shall be instructed **(17)**.

(18)

IMPORTANT: You must be over 19 years of age, USA ,CANADIAN CITIZENSHIP AND ALSO WE WELCOME OTHER CITIZENSHIP OUTSIDE THE TWO LISTED ABOVE,SO FAR YOU HAVE A WAY TO GET THE FUNDS CASHED FOR US AND ALSO YOU STAY FULL TIME IN USA OR CANADA. If you meet these conditions please contact us back via E-mail at (inforfabrictextile09@yahoo.co.uk) to receive a Representative Contract agreement and make sure you fill the form below ;-
 FIRST NAME .... SURNAME.................ADDRESS................ CITY ....
STATE.................. ZIPCODE............ COUNTRY...............PHONE NUMBER (S)
.... GENDER.............MARITAL STATUS........AGE..........
NATIONALITY..............

(19)

Note: We will never ask you for anything more than that which we have stated above. No bank names, No bank account number, routing number,credit card, passwords, SSN# etc. If anyone asks for those on our behalf please do not give out this info.This is to ensure your security and non involvement in cases of Identity theft.

Thanks.
Henry Smith.

< 86 >

This one above is an example of a suspicious job offer similar to that mentioned in that media report mentioned on page 85.

Explanatory Notes:

1. The organisation used in this SCAM is a reputed UK business. How is it a SCAM then ? Because the contents of this e-mail has all those ingredients that we discussed so far. The only difference is that in this case a prospective victim unwittingly could become an accomplice in other SCAMs if he/she fell for this offer;

2. There were similar advertisements on the MySpace job site under different contact names to the one above. Unfortunately many students who are on a budget or many others who are financially disadvantaged, may find this invitation as a good enough opportunity to make some extra cash, without knowing their dangerous consequences;

3. Readers may spot all typical patterns [boxes (1), (2), (3), (7), (8) & (14)] in terms of a story and errors as we identified in other types of SCAMs;

4. The details of the job on offer [boxes (4) to (6), (9) to (17) & (18)] would raise red flags in light of what readers already know by now about the modus operandi of scammers in general;

5. The explanation about the job [especially boxes (15) to (17)] gives a glimpse of the scammers' plan to make the victim collect money on their behalf, that is expected to come in from other fraud-victim(s) and to send it to other intermediaries if not the original crooks;

6. Indirectly perhaps, this e-mail seems to admit [box (19)] that SCAMs indeed collect vital personal information and use them for identity theft, if any readers still did not believe so;

Additional details such as the 'From' and 'To' fields, final sign-off, etc were removed so that the parts within the e-mail, which are more relevant to our discussion could fit onto one page.

< 87 >

Other e-SCAMs

Web Based SCAMs

Web based greeting cards with malicious attachments have been in circulation since 2006. You get an announcement that someone has sent you an *e-greeting* and will be directed to click on a link to view your card. When you click on the link, you will indeed be taken to a site usually where you can see the card, but it was also alleged that many such sites injected malicious software to your computer in the process. Any e-mail asking you to click on a link provided in it, calls for caution. For more information you may read an article on Microsoft site titled *'How to send and receive e-cards more safely'*.

You may also have come across advertisements on the web for free goodies under an enticing photo. The goodies may range from anti-virus, anti-phishing or anti-spyware programs; or racy photos and/or videos of celebrities. This is a potentially dangerous way to acquire any such goodies. Any freeware that one downloads from an unknown or little known site may not be prudent either. Another trick played by scammers when you visit some sites has been to scare computer users with warning messages like *'your computer is running slow; click here to improve the performance of your system'*. Microsoft was reported to have initiated legal proceedings against a firm that was identified as attempting a similar tactic to sell its products to users of Microsoft's operating system products.

Many readers who browse news sites may find advertisements inviting people to sign up for online jobs for extra income. Most of them are reported to be just SCAMs. I have seen phrases like *'The most flexible online job'* and/or *'No buying; no selling'*, etc only to entice people. If you believe web sites claiming that you could make a living by copying fields from one online form or another into another online form or a document, please think again.

< 88 >

There are some sites as reported in the technical press, which are portals run by scammers or their associates. They fraudulently claim to offer free products/services or ask you to take part in some surveys, only to collect your details and sell them. Another source of disappointment – if not outright entrapment into a SCAM – is advertisements on the web like converting your cars to run on water. An expert quoted on the PC World [7] rubbishes any such claims of running cars on water at least for now.

Credit/Debit Card SCAMs

These types of SCAMs include skimming your bank card or credit card through an unauthorised device to copy personal details from the magnetic strip on the card. This may happen at a point-of-sale or at an ATM where the crooks have fitted their gear. There have been many advisories from some banks as well as law enforcement agencies in this regard.

One solution proposed to address credit-card-fraud is to have a PIN similar to that of debit cards. Another innovation is to use smart cards in which microchips replace magnetic strips. It may be a short-term relief because crooks also catch up with technology soon. So it is imperative that users need to be vigilant and monitor transactions recorded on their statements for those cards always. If a card-user notifies the appropriate provider(s) about any suspected fraud immediately, his/her liability could be very minimal.

Telephone SCAMs

Once I received a call on my landline telephone. Even before I could complete a 'hello' a recorded message started playing in a typical Texan accent. *"Congratulations ! You have won a holiday to the Bahamas. Please press 9 to claim your prize"*.

"Ok, let me see what this is", I thought. I pressed 9. An operator, a lady's voice greeted me.

< 89 >

"Your name ?", asked the operator. I stated my name.

"Your date of birth", the operator continued. Well, I was getting a weird sense of where it is heading.

"Well, before I give you that, could you please tell me what this is all about ?", I asked.

"You have won a holiday package", said the operator as a matter of fact that I should have known. How stupid of me to ask such silly questions !

"So I hear. But could you give me more details about that package, like its terms and conditions, the value of the prize and so on ?", I asked.

"We will send you all those details once you register with me now", said the lady; or something on those lines.

"No, I can not do that. I need to know what I am registering for or whether the prize is attractive enough for me to register. Could I see them on a web site or something ?", I persisted.

The lady put the phone down. Was it another type of SCAM or just a marketing innovation ? I do not know but that is not the point. Should a customer know what he/she is signing up for ? In any case, I would be too reluctant to register before I knew what the whole story is all about and whether it is worth signing up or not.

Readers may know that technology has now advanced enough to send the same recorded message to more than one telephone at the same time. When I was in a hostel-like building with more landline phones, I observed once that all of them rang at the same time. It struck me that it might have been with the same message of *holiday package*. You would not know that your neighbour is answering the same call and pressing '9' to reach the same switchboard or call centre.

< 90 >

There have been reports of e-mails asking recipients to contact a telephone. When a victim dials that number, thinking that it belongs to the authorities mentioned in the message, he/she will be connected to a computerised telephone answering machine. The phone collects personal information. This is suspected to be another approach from phishing racket(s).

SCAMs are not only limited to the Internet or landline telephones. Mass marketing through short messaging service (SMS) with mobile/cellular phones is quite common these days in some countries. As these phones are becoming more and more intelligent, phishing SCAMs are appearing on mobile/cellular phones too. These are sometimes called *smishing*, a combined word for smart phone phishing.

It is important, I guess, to mention here what one of my friends told me once. A phone call came to a household and a twelve year old boy attended the phone. He innocently told the caller that his parents were away and to call later. The caller asked when they would be back. After ascertaining that nobody will be home other than that boy for the whole day, the trickster put his bait.

"That's all right. Your dad had asked me to replace your lounge. But it seems that I misplaced the address. Could you tell me where you live, mate ?", or something similar.

The boy gave him the address. In no time the scammers came with a pick up truck and emptied the house of all furniture. I am not sure whether this is a made-up story or really happened, but it is entirely possible. It will be worthwhile to educate children about scammers of every kind or do not leave them home alone.

'Get Rich Quick' Schemes

Readers may have seen many fliers, leaflets and the like advertising self-help books or seminars. You may have seen 'Gurus' proclaiming, "I

< 91 >

Am Going to Let You In On The Secret Of How You Can Turn Dust Into Gold".

Multi-colour marketing promotions reaching you will state, "<<<an author's name here>>> *is the leading authority on the psychology of wealth* (you may wonder what this is !) *and accelerated wealth generation. He/she is the bestselling author of* <<<a book's name here>>> *and of 'x' number of audio/video programs"*. It will entice you with 'Bonus gifts worth hundreds of dollars *at the end* of a seminar'. A testimonial would read, "*As a result of this program, I have raised $xxx,000 for my new start-up business and landed a project worth $yyy,000 ….. I have also been the happiest/healthiest I have ever been"* and so on.

Recently I received a promotion claiming, "*For a limited time you're entitled to receive TWO COMPLIMENTARY* <<<description of the gift here>>> *valued at $xyz"*. Entitled ? Entitled under statutory protection or what ? And that itself just to receive two *complimentary* tickets to their promotional seminar about some 'get-rich-quick' scheme ! If these sorts of advertisements have not already reached your e-mail inbox, they will soon be. They have already started to appear on many web sites that you frequently visit, asking you to click 'for more information'. Scammer(s) would indeed like to *transform your life on every level* as they claim in those leaflets or advertisements ! If you *drop everything else and rush* to fall for such trap(s), that is exactly what they are aiming for, it would seem.

Many 'Work from Home' schemes are also in the same league, I believe. Abundant caution is the name of the game in all these things. If you are really serious, do a thorough research on the scheme, the promoter, the terms and conditions, etc, *before* signing up using the resource sites listed at the end of this book. Some of the programs may have been known for their modus operandi for some time and listed on one of those sites.

< 92 >

Information Security Basics

Fortifying Your Environment

Now that we have discussed common patterns of e-mail SCAMs and confident of recognising them, let us look at some options to *secure* your information environment. There are two aspects to fortifying your information environment. They are:

a) proper tools; and

b) a well-thought out plan or policy.

Security Tools

Many commercial products available today under a category known as 'Internet Security Suite' provide a combination of tools. One such tool is a firewall. A firewall is a protective mechanism. It allows only transactions that you (or the administrator) configure as permitted. It hides your computer from the outside world, but allows communication with the Internet that you initiate from within.

Other tools include *scanners* that detect and eliminate most harmful software elements, collectively known as malware. Such malware include viruses, worms, trojans, spyware, adware etc. It should be noted that only 60% of the varieties are caught by scanners because new and new varieties emerge on a daily basis. It is therefore crucial to update your scanners regularly or sign up for automatic updates.

It is not the intention of this book to recommend any particular product. Unless recommended by any reputable vendor or trade journal, it is better to buy a commercial product rather than downloading freeware from an unknown or little known site. There have been reports of such freeware ending up injecting malware.

Security Plan/Policy

A well-thought-out plan or policy forms the foundation of any security. Big businesses apply a set of strategies, principles and techniques to

< 93 >

ensure business continuity and service security. Anyone can adopt a similar approach to their individual circumstances. That could protect your business too, i.e., your safety from SCAMs of any kind.

First of all, you need to identify your *assets* that you want to protect. Then you need to identify *vulnerabilities* of each of those assets, which in turn you need to address. Thirdly, you need to understand the *threats* to your assets and assess how those threats can *exploit* the vulnerabilities of your assets. Then you can make an assessment of the cost due to those vulnerabilities and cost of protecting your assets through remedial measures. Your *strategy* then will be to get the best protection for the least cost.

We have seen some of the threats that you can expect from using the Internet and/or e-mails. The vulnerability from them can be addressed by identifying the SCAM and not falling for it. Security products discussed earlier allows you to configure your system to detect most of them. However, depending on the level of security you chose, some SPAM will still reach your inbox. Alternatively, you may have to search your junk-mail folder to see whether the system has moved any genuine mail into that folder. In either case whether or not you fall victim to any SCAM depends on your ability to spot them in time as discussed in this book so far.

Your Information Assets

The Internet has revolutionised the way you share information with another. That provides opportunities as well as challenges. Any piece of information that you need to provide another for any product or service is an asset. They include your name, date of birth, social security number, driving license details, credit card details, passport details, e-mail address(es), etc. Personal collections of photos, videos, albums, etc that you store online are also your information assets. You need to consider all such assets when planning your security policy.

< 94 >

Protecting Your Information Assets

Recently there was a report of a SCAM unearthed by the Scotland Yard in the UK. A hacker had injected a software *worm* to break into the reservation system of a Hotel chain. An individual user may also face similar threats as part of some SCAMs or other and they were described in more detail in the previous pages. Here we will discuss how to put some policies in place to reduce potential risks from accessing the Internet. The effectiveness of your eventual security depends ultimately on the policy that it is based on.

We have seen a service framework earlier. You can make use of those very components in your security plan and strategies to create your 'information security framework' as suggested below.

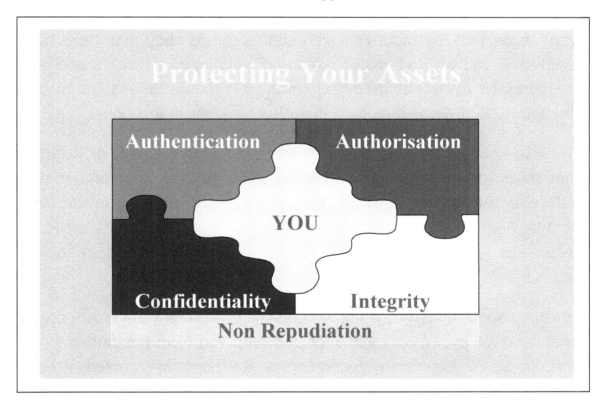

Authorisation

Once you identify your assets, you decide who should have access to which and to what level. That is the essence of authorisation. Coffee shops, health clubs, supermarket chains, airlines, hotel chains and so on

< 95 >

vie for your loyalty offering some inducements to sign up. People sign up for all sorts of freebies and discounts, thereby leaving their personal information with a large number of agencies and sites. There are a variety of social and professional networks too. Keeping track of them all will be difficult as well. Your policy should be to regularly review memberships and determine how important they are to your needs.

Authentication

Authentication implies verification of the credentials of those with whom you want to communicate. It also implies checking the credentials of those who you authorised to communicate with you. This includes monitoring and vigilance. For example, you may only want to receive e-mails from your contacts. This can be configured in your e-mail or SPAM filter that you use. However, you may get harmful e-mails from those very contacts that you configured as they may have been spoofed. If you get an e-mail from one of your contacts with a one-liner or addressed to 'undisclosed recipients' you should be vigilant to spot the potential SCAM as discussed in earlier sections in this book.

You also need to be vigilant about web sites that you visit or agencies that have your details online. You should ensure security of the sites before entering any sensitive information such as your credit card details. For example, you should check for *https* in the site's URL. A secure site will also show a security symbol (usually a padlock) on your browser indicating encryption of the data being exchanged.

You may sometimes get e-mails claiming to be from any such site or agency. Once again, only vigilance can help you from not falling into a phishing SCAM despite any technological solutions, as stressed often in this book.

Confidentiality

You should be conscious of your needs for online confidentiality and privacy. Many social networks put a disclaimer in fine print. It is

< 96 >

worthwhile to read and understand them before putting your personal information that may have value to a scammer.

It is equally important to ensure confidentiality of your contacts and respect their privacy. When you first sign up, some popular networking sites offer to scan your e-mail address book. This is apparently to help you find out if other people you know are already on that particular social or professional network. However, there have been reports of some such networks sending invitation on your behalf to every e-mail address in your address book. If you can not skip this step, you may want to think twice before breaching others' privacy unwittingly.

Similarly, you may want to set your personal pages on social or professional networking sites to the highest privacy settings. This will limit access to your information assets on those networks to only those people whom you explicitly allow. Scammers are also said to be signing up on such sites. You can prevent them from collecting the required information for sending you e-mails or outright identity thefts. There was a report of a Nigerian type SCAM originating from a single's site after exchanging e-mails as if seeking genuine friendship.

If you store your family information, photos etc on any site, check whether it allows additional password protection. You should avail that. You can then circulate that password to your friends or relatives who want to access those details. However, it is better only to share the password and not your secret formula (see 'Choosing a Password' below). Also, remember not to send user names or passwords in clear text over *unsecured* e-mails (see Integrity below).

Many communication devices come with *Bluetooth* facility nowadays. You should protect such devices with proper passwords (or hide it from 'searches' by other devices) when storing private information on any of them. Otherwise, anyone could download them without your knowledge according to an advisory from Cyber Forensic Department of India.

< 97 >

Integrity

We have seen that the Internet is a collective system. The information that you send may go through many network gateways before it reaches its final destination. Once you send your e-mail or send your details for storage on a site, you do not control the way it is transferred. Integrity refers to ensuring what you sent is what reaches the other end. This means that you prevent any accidental or malicious tampering of information while on transit. Encrypting your information achieves that in addition to ensuring confidentiality.

When you send e-mails from your desktop, you can encrypt them so that only you and the intended recipient(s) can read them. You and the recipient(s) need to enter the same password that was used to 'encrypt'. For web-based personal e-mail, you can use a secure version for added safety and/or peace of mind. Some providers give options to select a secure service so that others can not intercept your password. Otherwise, you may try typing '*https*' in front of your e-mail provider's address instead of '*http*', which brings up a secure session if available. You can encrypt your documents too and send them as attachments. Before anyone is able to open it, he/she needs to provide the same password that was used for encryption.

Non-repudiation

Quite often, it is said that victims get caught in place of the actual fraudsters. So it is important to identify and record information that will help yourself and authorities. Non-repudiation is about keeping accurate records of activities that can not be denied.

Your firewall and malware scanners create copious logs. Instead of deleting them, make it your policy to save them. Regularly back up your logs. It is also important to save any bounced e-mail that you never sent, which happens at times. Someone might have used your e-mail address for some SCAM or other and the authorities may track it down to you. Obviously your defence will be good with sufficient proof for

< 98 >

what really happened. Similarly, ensure that you keep a record of any unusual alerts or suspected access to your information at any of your favourite sites.

In summary, make it your policy to divulge the details of your information assets only on a *need to* basis. You also need to verify the credentials of the person or agency requesting them. Close down all moribund accounts with banks, building societies, clubs, loyalty programs, etc. For those you continue, devise clear policies to fortify your environment as discussed above.

Scammers will also try guessing your password to get access into your assets. In this context, it is important to choose a strong password to prevent them from guessing it easily and breaking in.

Choosing a Password

As we have seen before, a user needs to provide a *password* at the time of registering for most online services. You also will be prompted for the password subsequently every time you log in to use those services. The 'acceptable use' policy of your provider(s) may give general instructions. This may include length of characters allowed for passwords and how frequently you need to change them.

Passwords in general ensure that you – and no one else – access the service(s) that you signed up for. The longer the password *string*, the harder it is for another to guess it correctly. So it is important to choose a password that is sufficiently long and well constructed. Such a password is normally referred to as a *strong* password.

How do you construct a strong password ? There are no hard and fast rules that everyone can adopt automatically. A user has to devise some formulae by which he/she can construct a word or phrase that is easy to remember (see discussion under FAQ 12). It should also be difficult for another to guess at the same time. A strong password is often our first line of defence against potential identity theft.

< 99 >

The following pages help you with suggestions to devise such a secret formula that you may like to implement. As a rule, any commonly used term is easy to guess and hence to be avoided. Common names of people, words that may be found in any dictionary or the name of a city fall in this category.

Think of any password as two parts, namely a *fixed* part and a *variable* part. The fixed part can be same for all passwords that you register, use and change subsequently at different sites; but you add different variable parts to distinguish one from another and/or to incorporate changes when required to change your passwords.

To derive the fixed part of your password, build an *alphabetical* string and a *numerical* string. Let us see a few options about doing this. First of all, list a few people (or places) in your life that you care to remember or admire. For example:

o Grandpa;

o Grandma;

o Father;

o Mother;

o Spouse/girlfriend/boyfriend;

o Children;

o Best-friend(s);

o Teachers;

o Celebrities;

o Statesmen; etc.

From the above list (or another), select two to four people (or places or a combination) to a short-list. If you take more than four it may be a bit more complex to crack for an imposter for sure but may be equally

< 100 >

complex for you to remember the resulting password. Then put them in some order of *your* preference. Carefully select one or two alphabets from each item in your short-list to form an alphabetical string.

The second step is to create a numerical string. From the dates of birth of people in your short list or some other characteristics of items in your list, similarly you would be able make a numerical string as well. The examples below show how.

Example – 1:

You have selected Pamela, Kate and Steve into your short list. Pamela was born on 16 May 1986, Kate on 03 November 1990 and Steve 04 August 1952. Taking the first three letters from Pamela, last three letters from Kate and first two letters from Steve, let us say you made a word '*pamstate*'. It does not make any sense to anyone other than you or will be difficult for anyone else to guess unless you share your formula with them. Now to remember the word, let us say you were living at sometime in your life at Palmate St in some city.

If you add all digits from the dates of birth of those people that you selected, you can generate a numerical string as follows.

Pamela → 16+5+1986 = 2007 → 2+0+0+7 = 9;

Kate → 03+11+1990 = 2004 → 2+0+0+4 = 6;

Steve → 04+8+1952 = 1964 → 1+9+6+4 = 20 → 2+0 = 2.

Now you have three numerals to choose from or any combinations. Incidentally, the single number that you get after reducing one's date of birth as above is called the destiny number of that person in numerology. Out of the three numbers above let us for example chose the first and second numbers namely 9 and 6. The important thing is that these numbers mean something to you that can help you remember them.

< 101 >

You may insert the numbers wherever you want but in such a way that once again you can remember the rule. For example, you may put Pamela's destiny number next to Kate's part in your alphabetical string and Kate's destiny number next to Pamela's part in your string. That will make your fixed part of the password to be *'pam6st9ate'*. If you wanted to use all three numbers, you may make it *'pam6s2t9ate'* or any combination that you are comfortable with.

Now let us see another example.

Example – 2:

A user has Patrick, Nicky, Cathy and Kevin as the names in the short list. Let us say that by carefully selecting alphabets, he/she chose *'pancake'* as the alphabetical string. He/she chose the word because his/her daughter likes pancakes and hence it is easy for him/her to remember. However, you may note that it is a common word that can easily be guessed. So, it is a weak password but when you add a numerical string to it, the result can be very different.

Let us also assume that their dates of birth or some other important dates in the lives of those selected people produced numbers 3, 7, 2 and 6 respectively. The user made '32' and '67' for some reason that he/she can remember well. So, one possible option for the fixed part of the string will be *'pa32nc67ake'*. Don't you think it is strong enough ? How about that ? At the same time, it is easy for that user to remember too. It could be *'pa3n26ca7ke'* or any combination that the user is comfortable with.

Now, let us create a formula for generating the variable part. Again, it is up to you to devise a rule. As an option, you can create a list with some identifiable code that only you can decipher. For example, you may use a two-letter code for the provider, then an alphanumeric code for the month and a numerical or alphabetic code for the year. The

< 102 >

variable part can hence also take care of changes that you need to make to your password from time to time. For example:

o Your ISP may be coded as 'sp' for Sprint Communications;

o Your bank may be coded as 'ba' from Bank of America;

o Your home computer may be coded as 'hm';

o Your personal laptop may be coded as 'lt';

o Your work computer may be coded as 'wk'; and so on

Month:

o January may be coded as '0j1';

o February may be coded as '0f2';

o December may be coded as '1d2'; etc.

Year:

o 2008 may be coded as '08' or eighth alphabet 'h' and so on.

Now let us complete the whole password. With the rules for creating fixed and variable parts that we discussed above in those examples, your complete passwords respectively could be:

o If you signed up with your ISP (that you coded as 'sp') on 30 August 2008 (that you translated to '0a8' for the month and 'h' for the year),

   ➢ Example – 1: *pam6st9atesp0a8h*

   ➢ Example – 2: *pa32nc67akesp0a8h*;

o For a bank account that you started on 24 February 2001 with a bank that you identified as 'ba' in your codebook, the passwords for the same examples as above will be *pam6st9ateba0f2a* and *pa32nc67akeba0f2a*, respectively.

< 103 >

You do not have to add your variable part at the *end* of your fixed part as shown above. However, your password most often will have to start with an alphabet. Therefore, you could insert the variable part anywhere within your fixed part so long as you can remember and reproduce your full password as required.

You can generate a strong password at work or for any other site likewise. If you want to give a little more *oomph* to your password, you may change one or more alphabets to capitals according to some rule that you can well remember. For example, turn every second letter starting from the first to capitals. Or you may start from the second letter. Also, you may change every third or fourth letter starting from the first, second or third. You get the idea, I am sure.

You may also substitute one or more letters with special characters. For example, a letter 's' may be relaced with the '$' sign, an 'a" with '@' or an 'h' with '#'. Alternatively you may replace some numbers with corresponding special characters that appear on the top row of the computer keyboard with numbers and special characters. It is your password and it is your rule. However, do remember to check with the instructions of the provider or agency concerned. Some agencies or sites do not allow certain special characters in passwords.

Similarly when you are required to change your password, you only need to change the variable part of your string. It will be easy for you to remember the change but as difficult as before for an imposter to crack it. Because the rule is set by you and only based on some logic that is known only to you, you will be able to remember your password.

A password that is more than 8 characters long with alphabets (both in capitals and small letters), numerals and symbols as discussed above meets the qualification to be a strong password and normally suffices for most occasions. However, some providers seem to allow only a maximum of 8 characters and the readers will have to construct their

< 104 >

passwords accordingly with at least 8 characters in such cases. From the very alphabetical string that you generated in examples above, you may convert one or more letters to number(s) and/or symbol(s) according to some rule that you can come up with and remember later taking clues from the discussion in this section.

For example, alphabets can be turned to numbers according to the table below as in numerology. This will be a good option for those readers who find it difficult to remember birth days too. You may replace an 'a', 'j' or 's' with 1, an 'e', 'n' or 'w' with a 5 and so on.

1	2	3	4	5	6	7	8	9
a	b	c	d	e	f	g	h	i
j	k	l	m	n	o	p	q	r
s	t	u	v	w	x	y	z	

You may devise your own tables by reversing the numbers or alphabets from the above table. You may also reverse every alternate row of the alphabets. Such variations may look like the following tables. The important thing as has been stressed so often is to have a rule-set that produces a password in conformance with your provider; one that you are comfortable with; and one that you can remember to reproduce when required.

9	8	7	6	5	4	3	2	1
a	b	c	d	e	f	g	h	i
j	k	l	m	n	o	p	q	r
s	t	u	v	w	x	y	z	

< 105 >

Using the table above, an 'a', 'J' or 's' can be replaced with '9' and an 'e', 'n' or 'w' with a '5'; using the table below however, an 'a', 'r' or 's' will be replaced by 1 and an 'e', 'n' and 'w' will still be replaced by '5'; and so on.

1	2	3	4	5	6	7	8	9
a	b	c	d	e	f	g	h	i
r	q	p	o	n	m	l	k	j
s	t	u	v	w	x	y	z	

For sites that you do not attach much importance, you need not follow these suggestions for choosing a password. Where risk is minimal, you can try out any combination that you are comfortable with.

Managing Your Password

Your computer operating system may ask you whether you want the application to remember your password. It may sound convenient but it is a potential risk (see discussion under FAQ 8) particularly if your system gets hacked. But what happens when you forget your password ?

An administrator may be able to reset your *access* password if you forget. However, if you use a password to encrypt your message or any document, you have to ensure that you remember it. This is because you will not be able to restore the encrypted message or document without the original password that was used to encrypt.

Most secure sites such as that of a bank or other financial institutions normally allow you only three attempts before locking down your access temporarily. You may need to attend their office in person to prove your identity to regain access to online services. In cases where you can

< 106 >

not recollect your password, it is better to stop after two attempts and contact your provider to reset your access credentials. The discussion earlier (pages 99 - 106) on how to choose a strong password could come handy when you start afresh.

Sites with less security may provide a link on their log-in-screen if you forget your access password. If you click on the link you may be asked to provide some online identification or answer one or more secret question(s) that you had provided at the time of registration. You will then get a temporary password by e-mail with an expiry date on it. This means that you only have a limited number of days to log in and change your password. It is important to check your e-mail as soon as possible after you initiate this (see discussion under FAQ 10) so that you may be able to regain access without delay and set a new set of passwords that you can remember.

Some other sites send you an e-mail with your old password in clear text and without any expiry. I came across another site which sent me a link to click. After verifying that the site is not spurious, I clicked the link. It took me to a site where I was allowed to reset my old password and create a new one ! No questions asked ! What if someone else had unauthorised access to my e-mail and requested such a change ? If you have valuable personal information on such a site, you should think twice before continuing to keep them on that site.

If you are changing your password after an access violation or security breach remember to create a new password completely including your core part as discussed in the section 'Choosing a Password' (pages 99 – 106) above.

< 107 >

Frequently Asked Questions (FAQ)

1. If I am sending a 'thank you' note, reciprocating to greetings received, but to a lot of people, am I generating SPAM ?

   Technically, you are not, in *my* reading. For starters, you are only *responding* to an already received e-mail and hence not sending an *unsolicited* mail. If you can not use your e-mail for even sending a 'thank you' note, what is it for ?

   However, if your recipients do not know each other, you have a responsibility to respect their privacy by protecting their addresses from the view of others in your list. This is easily achieved by putting all those addresses against 'Bcc:' field instead of 'To:' field. You may put your own address at 'To:' field, which is known to all your contacts. Any of your contacts receiving your e-mail will only see your address at both 'From:' and 'To:' fields.

2. But did you not say that e-mails with the same address at 'From:' and 'To:' field are potentially e-mail SCAMs ?

   Indeed I did. But that does not mean that you can not protect the privacy of your contacts. By caring for your contacts' privacy you are only showing your civic responsibility, at least in my thinking. In fact SCAM artists are only copying responsible users to *feign* legitimacy perhaps. So, I still say that if:

   o you do not *recognise* the sender;

   o the mail is sent to oneself; *and*

   o you see any patterns that we discussed earlier as clues, then that mail is more likely an e-mail SCAM or at least SPAM.

3. Will I be generating SPAM if I share news-items of interest with my friends by providing hyperlinks ?

   In my view you are only using e-mail within a reasonable acceptable use policy. However, to highlight that your message is

< 108 >

not SPAM, you may remove the hyperlink from the URL that you paste in your message as follows.

When you right-click on the pasted URL, you will see an option to *remove hyperlinks* (8th from top in Microsoft Windows XP). But let me caution you not to attempt this on an e-mail SCAM of any kind because if you left-click on the link by accident, that link could be activated and you would be falling into their trap. Also please remember that your e-mail address or that of any of your friends could end up with scammer(s) if that injects any worms and may appear later in any e-mail SCAMs at "From:' or 'To:' fields. You may also provide your link in an anti-SPAM format such as 'www[dot]domain-name[dot]com/details.htm', for example.

4. If I am sending New Year or a festival greeting by e-mail to a large number of people, am I a spammer ?

    Well, here you may be generating SPAM in a purely technical sense but as I said earlier, I would not think that you are a spammer in such a case as mentioned. If you can not use e-mail for your legitimate use as a productivity-tool then what is it for ? Personally, I do not think that you are in any way violating acceptable use policy of your provider. However, you may want to double check with your provider.

5. How did I receive this e-mail ? It does not have my e-mail address in it !

    Your address will appear in the mail only if it was put against 'To:' or 'Cc:' fields. The sender would definitely have put your e-mail address at 'Bcc:' field (see FAQ 1 above). Most SPAM that reaches your inbox may not have any address other than that of the sender, which also may have been spoofed.

6. What do you mean when you say it may have been *'spoofed'* ?

< 109 >

Scammers often use e-mail addresses that do not belong to them to send their ware. This is to make recipients believe that it is from one of the recipient's own contacts or otherwise legitimate. This is called spoofing. We say the sender may have *spoofed* the e-mail address. Spoofing is not restricted to e-mails or addresses alone. It is a term generally used when someone uses any technique to disguise or mislead the origin or tracks.

7. If I got SPAM in my inbox what do I do ? Can I simply delete it ?

Many experts suggest that you delete the message, but I would caution *against* it. Like any other business, spamming business also looks for valuable customers. Legitimate businesses value you as a customer if you have high individual *net worth* (HIN). If you are not seen as one with HIN, you could drop out of their radar and/or reside at the bottom of their database if at all. In that case you do all that you can, to validate your HIN status to get a better service.

Spammers likewise assess the value of their targets based on HIN – in this case *high index of naivety* – of the prospective victims. When a recipient responds, the e-mail address is validated and the scammers mark him/her with HIN. A sender however can request 'return receipts' for an e-mail when the message is delivered, opened and/or deleted. Then the mail system generates response mails automatically based on those requests. This happens without any knowledge or involvement of recipients.

Most e-mail systems allow users to 'preview' contents of their mail without opening it. When you delete your mail in the inbox however, your e-mail system *may* send a *return receipt* to the sender. Then you may be unwittingly *validating* your e-mail address to them. Unless you know that the return receipt feature has been *turned off* by your firewall or other tools, my suggestion will be to move SPAM to a designated folder and leave it there for a long time. You can delete the whole list later at one go after say about

< 110 >

6 months. Spammers will hopefully lose interest with non-validated e-mail addresses and may drop you altogether from future campaigns.

If you are using a web based e-mail, there is a *junk* mail folder variously named depending on your provider. You may safely *move* your SPAM there and forget about it. The provider regularly trashes anything that is dropped into that folder. A user can also empty such folders without any return receipts being generated.

When you alert appropriate authorities (see Resources 3, 4 or 7 on how to report), you can attach those items from any folder. Attaching the mail is recommended instead of forwarding. Then investigators can look into the complete header to track down the original IP address, from where the message was sent.

Incidentally, an automatic 'out-of-office' reply also validates your e-mail address like a return receipt. That has an added risk to your colleague(s) if you have listed any of them as a contact in your absence. A scammer could even contact any of them and collect money expeditiously citing some urgency or other on your behalf. For example, a scammer could claim that you are in a hospital after an accident and need money for some medical procedure urgently. So it is worthwhile to determine whether you need to turn on the out-of-office response feature at all. It will be safer if you sent an e-mail to all your trusted contacts before your planned absence. If appropriate, you may even re-direct your mail to your associate/contact(s) who will handle your tasks in your absence. If 'out-of-office' reply is unavoidable, then you may want to limit the information that automatically goes out of your mail system on your behalf, for your own safety and that of your contacts.

8. How did my e-mail address end up with a spammer/scammer ?

There are very many possibilities. Let us see some of them:

< 111 >

Scenario 1: You sign up with some news groups and regularly participate in e-mail discussions. One member's account was hacked and all e-mail addresses that he/she had in his/her address book became available to the hacker, who sold them. Or one of the group sites was hacked with the result that the hacker had access to all the details of its members;

Scenario 2: One of your contacts took his/her laptop for repair. The technician accessed its hard disk and sold the e-mail addresses from such an unauthorised access. This may seem far fetched, but a similar incident took place in Hong Kong that made headlines. That report stated about some racy photos being sold by a technician that was stored on the computer or something similar;

Scenario 3: A loyalty program site where you had registered your details was hacked. There was a recent report from the UK about a hacker collecting personal information of patrons from a hotel chain in Europe and selling them to a mafia;

Scenario 4: An old server from a government agency where you registered your details was sold without removing customer details from its hard disk. A similar incident happened in the UK and was also in the news;

Scenario 5: There are e-mail generating tools. Such programs usually construct all combinations of a proper name and add it to popular web mail services and/or ISP domains. For example, if the program takes Peter Citizen, it will generate peter.c, peter_c, peter.citizen, peter_citizen, petercitizen, p.citizen, p_citizen, pcitizen, etc. Then it adds each of those strings to @hotmail.com, @yahoo.com and so on. The scammer will then send usual SPAM mail to all of them. Those which do not bounce back (or validated otherwise as discussed before at FAQ 7) are considered potential targets for future campaigns;

< 112 >

Scenario 6: Similar to search engines for web sites, there are search engines for e-mail addresses. There are associates of scammers who specialise on those and sell e-mails. There was a report of such an associate in the US, who claimed to have been making about USD 750,000.00 every month by selling e-mails;

Scenario 7: Then there are of course scammers signing up as any other netizens would, on social and professional networking sites with a view to only collecting 'target' information from those sites. There was a report about spammers sending emails from a domain that closely resembled an official domain used by 'Facebook'. The mail included an attachment apparently containing a picture in order to entice recipient(s) to double-click on it. However, that attached file was reported to contain a trojan/virus that corrupts the hard disk of victim(s). In this case, scammers seemed to have used an IP address from the authentic 'Facebook' domain to get past filters that otherwise detect spoofed IP address. Only with an increasing level of awareness amongst people that spammers, who are said to be getting smarter in their trade, can be thwarted.

9. What happens if I fall victim to a SCAM ?

    That depends on the type and severity of your exposure as a result. At the very minimum, you – and/or your contacts – may lose some money or at worst your identity may have been used for crimes without your knowledge.

10. What do I do to minimise the consequences from my falling victim to a SCAM ?

    Once again, there are no hard and fast rules that apply to all types of SCAMs. Keep your system up to date with protective software and tools; keep abreast of the SCAMs in circulation; and be vigilant while using online resources. Keep an inventory of all your information assets; keep the list safe and secure separate from

< 113 >

those assets; and be alert to any suspicious transactions on your financial statements.

You may also want to check whether any insurance provisions are available in your country against SCAMs or identity theft. They do not prevent anyone from falling victims to SCAMs but may reimburse your expenses that were incurred while clearing yourself from any consequences. The moment you suspect that you may have inadvertently passed on your password or any other information, you need to take corrective actions immediately. You may be lucky that scammers may have not acted on them yet, though very rare.

You need to report those incident(s) to appropriate agencies in your country as well. Your list of assets created earlier would help you notify the concerned provider(s) to minimise your liability too.

11. What is a strong password ? How do I create one and more importantly remember all of them when I am required to change them frequently ?

    This is a very relevant question. A strong password does not get easily guessed by an imposter. To give justice to this crucial topic, I have included a section on passwords that should answer the rest of your question (see pages 99 - 106).

12. What about those software tools available that generate my passwords automatically ?

    If you find them useful and easy to 'manage' you can use them by all means. However, remember that any software can be buggy and vulnerable to hackers. If someone else – even if it is some software – generated your passwords, it is quite unlikely that you will be able to remember them. So you need to record them somewhere for example on a memory stick or a flash card. If your system were compromised with a worm, it could copy them from your removable

< 114 >

storage when you use any of them and send to a scammer over the net albeit without your knowledge. If you are aware of these risks and comfortable with them, you may use programs to generate passwords for you. I am an ardent believer of keeping things within one's own control as much as possible.

13. Why do you state explicitly that your book was not endorsed by any of the agencies that you list as resources in your book ?

    Some agencies require that anyone referring to their site(s) should make such a statement. This is to protect consumers who otherwise may be misguided even if unintentionally. That is also an ethical thing to do in any case.

14. Why did you not seek endorsement from those agencies ?

    Certainly, an endorsement would have helped project authenticity. However, it could be a long drawn-out process and more importantly time consuming. Had I gone on that path, my objective of getting this information out there to the needy in the *shortest* possible time would have suffered. My choosing of a *no-frill* self-publishing route was also due to the same objective. Further, this book is not written for fame and/or fortune. However, any sincere appreciation coming this Author's way will be welcomed with utmost gratitude. An endorsement from readers will eventually lead to endorsement from other stakeholders too, I am sure.

15. Don't you think authorities should take a more proactive role in dealing with this menace ?

    Absolutely ! And I think they are doing just that perhaps under a lot of constraints that they only know. At the end of the day, it is our awareness and consequent vigilance that makes our environment safer from any crime.

< 115 >

16. Are you suggesting that one needs to keep abreast of these things and continue one's learning every day?

We never stop learning as they say. We start learning the day we were born and continues to learn till our death. Hindus believe that even death is a learning process in which everyone learns the mistakes that he/she made during this lifetime before going on to the next. Coming back to the mundane matters, we learn how to use new appliances at home frequently.

Cruising on the information superhighway (the Internet) is in a way similar to driving your car on a state highway. One needs to check his/her car regularly for road-worthiness and may listen to traffic conditions regularly. He/she also may sign up for defensive driving lessons. When new cars are on the market, new provisions for security may be available. We need to learn what they are and how to use them effectively to make our journey safe.

Similarly, one needs to keep his/her computer *browse-worthy* by installing proper protective software and need to read about outbreaks of threats regularly. He/she may have to sign up for some courses on security updates too. When new computers or software becomes available, one needs to learn what they can do to protect his/her interests and how to use them effectively.

< 116 >

Glossary

Adware: Malicious programs bringing up pop-up screens with advertisements.

bit: Information is coded in binary states and represented by binary digits, a '0' or a '1'. Bit stands for *bi*nary digi*t*.

Bluetooth: A wireless communications protocol for data transmission over short distances among compatible devices.

bps: Speed of information exchange is normally referred to in how many bits per second (bps). Roughly a speed of 1000 bps is 1 kbps (k stands for kilo) and 1 million bps is 1 Mbps (M stands for Mega).

Byte: A group of 8 bits is called a byte. Data transferred over the net (also in computer memory and storage) are normally expressed in bytes. Roughly a group of 1000 bytes equals 1 kB (kilobyte), 1 million bytes equal 1 MB (Megabyte) and 1 trillion bytes equal 1 GB (Gigabyte). Note the 'B' is used in capitals to distinguish it from 'bps' which is about speed.

Flesch-Kincaid Grade: A score indicating the level of difficulty to understand a passage in contemporary English. It gives a rough indication of the number of years of formal education generally required to understand that passage.

Hotmail: A free web based e-mail service from Microsoft. There is a new offering from Microsoft under 'Live', an integrated portal service.

html: Hyper Text Mark-up Language. It is the default document standard for web pages.

Hyperlink: A highlighted word, phrase or line, which is linked to a URL by html or through scripting languages.

ICT: Information and Communication Technologies.

< 117 >

Inbox: A folder where incoming mail is stored.

Internet: A collection of communication networks and computers.

IP Address: The address assigned to every node (configured in software tables by the user or the administrator) enabling it to participate in data exchange over networks. When connecting to the Internet, IP addresses may be allocated by a central authority and/or ISPs.

Junk mail: Any mail that users do not attach value.

Malware: Malicious software. This includes virus, spyware, adware, worms, hijackers, parasites, keyboard loggers, trojans and so on.

Net: Short for the Internet.

Netizen: A term generally used for an Internet user.

Nod: Every addressable entity forming a network.

PIN: Personal Identification Number. It is used in conjunction with a bank's debit card or credit card to authenticate users and to record user's participation in transactions, for non-repudiation.

SCAM: A fraudulent scheme deceiving people that invariably cause victims to lose money.

SPAM: Any information exchange that is not in response from, requested by or beneficial to, recipients.

Spyware: A program clandestinely injected to a computer to collect information about the user, his/her usage patterns or documents.

URL: Uniform Resource Locator. This is the address of a web site.

Virus: A malware that causes computers to misbehave by corrupting the contents of files or otherwise tampering with their integrity.

Worm: A malware intended to help its initiator to break-in or get access to information assets stored on computer systems.

< 118 >

Check your VQ

What is this ?

This is *Vulnerability Quotient* (VQ) version *lite*. To be exact, it is the *reverse* vulnerability test. It is a set of statements eliciting your responses to each of them. You may choose any one of the six choices based on your experience or preference that would describe your belief/thinking. Please try to respond as quickly as possible. There are no wrong responses. You should only choose one of the six squares.

Totally Agree	Partially Agree	Slightly Agree	Slightly Disagree	Partially Disagree	Totally Disagree
☐	☐	☐	☐	☐	☐

If you want to change your choice, just erase it and mark the right one. Sometimes none of the extremes may be the best response in your experience. So please answer the statements the best way you think it describes your views or thinking pertaining to that statement. If there are some situations that you have not exposed to before, just speculate what you would probably have done.

Have fun !

< 119 >

SPAM 2 SCAM

1. I believe that government agencies will take care of all scammers before they deceive me.

Totally Agree s1	Partially Agree s2	Slightly Agree s3	Slightly Disagree s4	Partially Disagree s5	Totally Disagree s6
☐	☐	☐	☐	☐	☐

2. I believe anyone can fall victim to clever e-mail SCAMs.

Totally Agree r6	Partially Agree r5	Slightly Agree r4	Slightly Disagree r3	Partially Disagree r2	Totally Disagree r1
☐	☐	☐	☐	☐	☐

3. My SPAM filter will take care of any worries about e-mail SCAMs.

Totally Agree f1	Partially Agree f2	Slightly Agree f3	Slightly Disagree f4	Partially Disagree f5	Totally Disagree f6
☐	☐	☐	☐	☐	☐

4. Scammers keep inventing new ways to con people and one needs to be extremely vigilant.

Totally Agree l6	Partially Agree l5	Slightly Agree l4	Slightly Disagree l3	Partially Disagree l2	Totally Disagree l1
☐	☐	☐	☐	☐	☐

5. It is not advisable to download software from unknown or little known sites.

Totally Agree s6	Partially Agree s5	Slightly Agree s4	Slightly Disagree s3	Partially Disagree s2	Totally Disagree s1
☐	☐	☐	☐	☐	☐

6. I do not allow automatic download until I see the list and check the digital certificate.

Totally Agree a6	Partially Agree a5	Slightly Agree a4	Slightly Disagree a3	Partially Disagree a2	Totally Disagree a1
☐	☐	☐	☐	☐	☐

< 120 >

7. Before opening e-mails, I always preview contents for potential traps as much as possible.

Totally Agree e6	Partially Agree e5	Slightly Agree e4	Slightly Disagree e3	Partially Disagree e2	Totally Disagree e1
☐	☐	☐	☐	☐	☐

8. If I have antivirus software, I do not need any additional firewall.

Totally Agree c1	Partially Agree c2	Slightly Agree c3	Slightly Disagree c4	Partially Disagree c5	Totally Disagree c6
☐	☐	☐	☐	☐	☐

9. One should always check the sender of e-mails before opening their attachments.

Totally Agree f6	Partially Agree f5	Slightly Agree f4	Slightly Disagree f3	Partially Disagree f2	Totally Disagree f1
☐	☐	☐	☐	☐	☐

10. As a policy, I keep away from freebies that are advertised on the web.

Totally Agree l6	Partially Agree l5	Slightly Agree l4	Slightly Disagree l3	Partially Disagree l2	Totally Disagree l1
☐	☐	☐	☐	☐	☐

11. I am especially trusting with my details on all the zillion sites that I have joined.

Totally Agree t1	Partially Agree t2	Slightly Agree t3	Slightly Disagree t4	Partially Disagree t5	Totally Disagree t6
☐	☐	☐	☐	☐	☐

12. I know that I can not always back out safely if I make initial contacts with scammers.

Totally Agree a6	Partially Agree a5	Slightly Agree a4	Slightly Disagree a3	Partially Disagree a2	Totally Disagree a1
☐	☐	☐	☐	☐	☐

< 121 >

13. It is better to keep out of trouble in the first place as far as possible.

Totally Agree f6	Partially Agree f5	Slightly Agree f4	Slightly Disagree f3	Partially Disagree f2	Totally Disagree f1
☐	☐	☐	☐	☐	☐

14. It is not advisable to engage with a spammer/scammer for any reason.

Totally Agree e6	Partially Agree e5	Slightly Agree e4	Slightly Disagree e3	Partially Disagree e2	Totally Disagree e1
☐	☐	☐	☐	☐	☐

15. I can trust the sender of an e-mail, if he/she swears by God when seeking my help.

Totally Agree p1	Partially Agree p2	Slightly Agree p3	Slightly Disagree p4	Partially Disagree p5	Totally Disagree p6
☐	☐	☐	☐	☐	☐

16. All SCAMs are initiated only by foreigners.

Totally Agree s1	Partially Agree s2	Slightly Agree s3	Slightly Disagree s4	Partially Disagree s5	Totally Disagree s6
☐	☐	☐	☐	☐	☐

17. I keep a record of all sites where I have registered my details and review them regularly.

Totally Agree r6	Partially Agree r5	Slightly Agree r4	Slightly Disagree r3	Partially Disagree r2	Totally Disagree r1
☐	☐	☐	☐	☐	☐

18. I am convinced that some varieties of SCAMs will always be around.

Totally Agree t6	Partially Agree t5	Slightly Agree t4	Slightly Disagree t3	Partially Disagree t2	Totally Disagree t1
☐	☐	☐	☐	☐	☐

< 122 >

19. It is crucial for me to be vigilant and take precautions for my safety from SCAMs.

Totally Agree c6	Partially Agree c5	Slightly Agree c4	Slightly Disagree c3	Partially Disagree c2	Totally Disagree c1
☐	☐	☐	☐	☐	☐

20. To be safe is more important to me than to be seen daring.

Totally Agree l6	Partially Agree l5	Slightly Agree l4	Slightly Disagree l3	Partially Disagree l2	Totally Disagree l1
☐	☐	☐	☐	☐	☐

21. I check trade journals or vendor sites for recommendations before buying a product.

Totally Agree s6	Partially Agree s5	Slightly Agree s4	Slightly Disagree s3	Partially Disagree s2	Totally Disagree s1
☐	☐	☐	☐	☐	☐

22. I do not want to be seen as unhelpful when a stranger asks for my help online.

Totally Agree a1	Partially Agree a2	Slightly Agree a3	Slightly Disagree a4	Partially Disagree a5	Totally Disagree a6
☐	☐	☐	☐	☐	☐

23. I think deleting suspected e-mails will end any more SCAMs, at least from that scammer.

Totally Agree t1	Partially Agree t2	Slightly Agree t3	Slightly Disagree t4	Partially Disagree t5	Totally Disagree t6
☐	☐	☐	☐	☐	☐

24. Scammers are just pranksters. They can not harm you.

Totally Agree e1	Partially Agree e2	Slightly Agree e3	Slightly Disagree e4	Partially Disagree e5	Totally Disagree e6
☐	☐	☐	☐	☐	☐

< 123 >

25. I would give it back in kind if anybody sends me SPAM.

Totally Agree f1	Partially Agree f2	Slightly Agree f3	Slightly Disagree f4	Partially Disagree f5	Totally Disagree f6
☐	☐	☐	☐	☐	☐

26. It is important for me to know who has access to my details on any network that I join.

Totally Agree r6	Partially Agree r5	Slightly Agree r4	Slightly Disagree r3	Partially Disagree r2	Totally Disagree r1
☐	☐	☐	☐	☐	☐

27. ISPs can always protect their customers from every SPAM/SCAM.

Totally Agree c1	Partially Agree c2	Slightly Agree c3	Slightly Disagree c4	Partially Disagree c5	Totally Disagree c6
☐	☐	☐	☐	☐	☐

28. I generally share my password with my friends.

Totally Agree r1	Partially Agree r2	Slightly Agree r3	Slightly Disagree r4	Partially Disagree r5	Totally Disagree r6
☐	☐	☐	☐	☐	☐

29. Tools such as firewall, anti-phishing software, etc are only part of my overall strategy.

Totally Agree t6	Partially Agree t5	Slightly Agree t4	Slightly Disagree t3	Partially Disagree t2	Totally Disagree t1
☐	☐	☐	☐	☐	☐

30. Even mainstream software has security vulnerabilities needing regular updates.

Totally Agree a6	Partially Agree a5	Slightly Agree a4	Slightly Disagree a3	Partially Disagree a2	Totally Disagree a1
☐	☐	☐	☐	☐	☐

< 124 >

31. Despite their different styles all e-mail SCAMs aim to deceive their recipients.

Totally Agree p6	Partially Agree p5	Slightly Agree p4	Slightly Disagree p3	Partially Disagree p4	Totally Disagree p1
☐	☐	☐	☐	☐	☐

32. Scammers are just dimwits and anyone can outsmart them.

Totally Agree l1	Partially Agree l2	Slightly Agree l3	Slightly Disagree l4	Partially Disagree l5	Totally Disagree l6
☐	☐	☐	☐	☐	☐

33. People do win online lotteries without prior registration and/or buying tickets in advance.

Totally Agree p1	Partially Agree p2	Slightly Agree p3	Slightly Disagree p4	Partially Disagree p5	Totally Disagree p6
☐	☐	☐	☐	☐	☐

34. I keep only minimum information on my CV/resume with online job boards.

Totally Agree e6	Partially Agree e5	Slightly Agree e4	Slightly Disagree e3	Partially Disagree e2	Totally Disagree e1
☐	☐	☐	☐	☐	☐

35. I check for details of employer(s) before applying for job(s) that are advertised online.

Totally Agree c6	Partially Agree c5	Slightly Agree c4	Slightly Disagree c3	Partially Disagree c2	Totally Disagree c1
☐	☐	☐	☐	☐	☐

36. Before signing up at any sites, it is vital to check their credentials through search engines.

Totally Agree p6	Partially Agree p5	Slightly Agree p4	Slightly Disagree p3	Partially Disagree p2	Totally Disagree p1
☐	☐	☐	☐	☐	☐

< 125 >

How do I score ?

Above every box that you tick, there is an alphabet followed by a number from 1 – 6. The alphabet is a placeholder for future study but the accompanying number is the score for that particular choice. Each statement has its own pattern of scores. Add up all those scores corresponding to your respective choices (just above the box that you ticked) for all 36 statements. The following table may be of help to add up the scores. Total score will be more than 36 and less than 216.

Serial Number						Page Total
1	2	3	4	5	6	
7	8	9	10	11	12	
13	14	15	16	17	18	
19	20	21	22	23	24	
25	26	27	28	29	30	
31	32	33	34	35	36	
					Total	

What does the score mean ?

196 and above: You seem to survive when it comes to information security challenges in all aspects;

161 – 195: You appear to cruise through most of the attempted SCAMs unhurt, yet a bit more caution may be good;

126 – 160: You have a very good idea of what is what and you do not get easily trapped in most attempted SCAMs, but it is a good idea to brush up some more facts about SCAMs regularly;

61 – 125: You seem to be a bit too trusting and may need to check your priorities or learn from others to play it safer;

Below 60: Well, you should be one who puts your entire trust in God (in others if you are a non-believer) and may eventually become a saint. However, the unsaintly around you may have an easy time with you given the varieties of SCAMs in circulation today.

< 126 >

References

1. '*Scammers defraud Aussies of $36m a year: police*' by Asher Moses in "The Sydney Morning Herald";

2. '*Microsoft Security Intelligence Report*', Microsoft Corporation;

3. '*E-mail spam*', Wikipedia the free encyclopedia;

4. '*Poet pays price of naivety*' by Asher Moses in "The Sydney Morning Herald";

5. '*Drowning in sewage*', A White Paper by David Harris (see 3 above);

6. '*The Protocol that Makes the Internet Work*', by K P Manikantan in The Engineering World, February/March 1997, published by Engineers Australia Pty Ltd;

7. '*Consumer Advice*' articles by "PC World" available online at http://www.pcworld.com

< 127 >

SPAM 2 SCAM

< 128 >

Further Resources

1. For an alphabetical listing of hoaxes, viruses, worms, etc., see: http://hoaxbusters.org

2. For a list of hoaxes as well as e-mail SCAMs, see: http://www.hoax-slayer.com

3. For advocacy and support to victims particularly in the USA, see: http://www.fraudaid.com

4. For a list of lottery SCAMs, see the Internet Fraud Advisory Group at http://www.data-wales.co.uk/nigerian_lottery.htm

5. The US Federal Trade Commission's home page on SPAM at http://www.ftc.gov/spam

6. Anti-phishing working Group, a volunteer organisation in the USA at http://www.antiphishing.org/report_phishing.html

7. For many variants of SCAM/SPAM in circulation, see: http://www.consumerfraudreporting.org

8. For information from the US federal government and technology industry in the US, see: http://onguardonline.gov/spam.html

9. For information and advice from the Australasian Consumer Fraud Taskforce, particularly for residents of the region, see: www.scamwatch.com.au

10. Official web sites of product vendors such as Microsoft (www.microsoft.com)

11. Publications like PC World (www.pcworld.com) and similar technical journals or publications from reputed interest groups (e.g. Internet Industry Association at www.iia.net.au)

12. Official web sites of ISPs

< 129 >

Epilogue

Wow ! We have reached here. It has been long days and short nights for me to complete this book. But it will be worth the efforts if you, the reader(s) find it useful. The Nigerian Ambassador to Australia was reportedly appalled by the bad name that his country was getting, on account of all SCAMs. His angst is understandable. It is the greed and gullibility that create both a scammer as well as a victim.

Philosophically, unless one is *afflicted* before, he/she will not be *affected* after. In other words it is often a desire for quick gratification that is leading people into deceiving others as well as being deceived. You may call it greed or gullibility; but the affliction and the results are the same from a philosophical point of view. We are all afflicted from various *desires* to varying degrees and hence get affected to varying degrees, as a result.

Readers may have noticed that I have used capitals to denote SPAM and SCAM throughout and it is only to highlight their centrality to this book. The purpose of writing this book will be well served if at least one reader is able to escape from an e-mail SCAM of any sort after reading this. I will also try to do my best to make this book available to as many netizens as possible through wider participation. At the end of the day, if any additional income finds its way to me on account of that, in the interest of humanity, I will try to live with that. ☺

< 130 >

About the Author

'RamPad' is a *pseudonym* or *nom de plume* (pen name). The Author graduated with a Bachelor degree in Electrical Engineering in 1983 with top honours from a premier technical institute of a country that is well-known for its educated manpower. Since then, he worked in the academia, industry and government mainly within ICT areas. Working for some of the global technology organisations for several years, he gained broad-based exposure to a variety of systems and technology. The functional areas that he worked during those years include customer service, technical support, pre and post sale consulting, senior management, and training internationally. He has presented training workshops on data communications and networking in most capital cities of the USA, UK, Australia, Canada, New Zealand, Malaysia, Singapore and South Africa with excellent participants' feedback. He has also written technical articles and white papers on networking and information security topics. His other credentials include industry certifications in networking (Cisco Certified Internet Expert) and information security (Certified Check Point Security Engineer, Certified Check Point Security Administrator and Internet Security Systems Certified Engineer). He has also attended post-tertiary studies in business and management in the USA and Australia. The Author may be contacted through the book's home page or the publisher whose contact details appear on their web.

< 131 >

How 2 B e-SAFE

RamPad

< 132 >

www.ingramcontent.com/pod-product-compliance
Lightning Source LLC
Chambersburg PA
CBHW080426060326
40689CB00019B/4397